SOPHIE HEAWOOD

Sophie Heawood was born and raised in Yorkshire, where she never quite mastered the accent. She studied Spanish and Portuguese at university, where she also never quite mastered the accents, and dropped out of her degree to work on the door of nightclubs. Her parents were thrilled. She now lives in Hackney, East London, with her daughter and their dog. Sophie has written for many publications including *The Times, Guardian, Observer* and *Vogue*.

SOPHIE HEAWOOD

The Hungover Games

VINTAGE

1 3 5 7 9 10 8 6 4 2

Vintage is part of the Penguin Random House group of companies whose addresses can be found at global.penguinrandomhouse.com

Penguin
Random House
UK

Copyright © Sophie Heawood

Sophie Heawood has asserted her right to be identified as the author of this Work in accordance with the Copyright, Designs and Patents Act 1988

First published in Vintage in 2021
First published in hardback by Jonathan Cape in 2020

penguin.co.uk/vintage

A CIP catalogue record for this book is available from the British Library

ISBN 9781784707644 (B format)

Printed and bound in Great Britain by Clays Ltd, Elcograf S.p.A.

The authorised representative in the EEA is Penguin Random House Ireland, Morrison Chambers, 32 Nassau Street, Dublin D02 YH68.

Penguin Random House is committed to a sustainable future for our business, our readers and our planet. This book is made from Forest Stewardship Council® certified paper.

MIX
Paper from
responsible sources
FSC® C018179

For my mother and my daughter – thank you both for bringing me up.

You might want to stop reading here though.

Author's note

This book is based on my own personal experience and my memories of a certain period of my life. Other people who were close to me at the time may, of course, remember things differently, and some names have been excluded or changed for reasons of privacy. This is because this is not a book about the individuals I have described, but about my own experiences and how they shaped my life.

'Love is the extremely difficult realisation that something other than oneself is real.'

Iris Murdoch, 'The Sublime and the Good'

Prelude
There's something
I haven't explained

I 'm in a bar with a man whom we'll call Dom. I met him on a dating app, which we'll call Linger. This app serves to bring together people who might want to fall in love, or have sex, or simply message each other intermittently over several days before becoming incandescent with rage and then fatally resigned to the time it is taking for the other person to reply. Dom replied, though, and when I asked what he was up to he said something about not being sure if he currently had profound existential ennui or just a hangover, and I thought, yeah, you'll do.

Dom looked nice in the photos too, but mainly because I had scrolled through 268 other men before getting to Dom, and unlike the 268, Dom wasn't standing in front of a large shiny motorbike, parachuting from a light aircraft, or inexplicably befriending a Bengal tiger with a

glazed expression. Dom was unaccompanied by conspicuous consumption, airborne vehicles or ferocious animals
– not that these are things I am opposed to, it's just that,
when used in profile pictures, they tend to indicate the
presence of a wanker.

He had scruffy hair and the slightly serious face of
someone who was far too young for me, but then how
would he know that, when my profile said that I was
twenty-eight, which had started as a joke but now become
true in its own way. I had set this profile up from my
new life, in which I thought it was too embarrassing to
be doing this, so I made it look like as if my old life was
still going strong, as if nothing had changed.

And now it's closing time in the bar and Dom wants
to come back to mine. Which is a bit awkward, but damn
it, maybe it'll be okay, I think. I ask about where he lives,
and he reminds me that it's a few miles away and didn't
I already say that this place was my local? And I say,
well, all right. So I take him back to the house and tell
him he has to be super quiet on the stairs because there's
someone asleep in that room, and someone else asleep in
that room, and here's my bedroom, shhhh. We stumble
onto my bed together and I'm already starting to sober
up, just as he's starting to be incoherently loving, pawing,
lost, and I wonder about the idea that alcohol makes men
violent because it seems to turn all the ones I meet into
water. It's me who turns into noise, shouting over the
top of myself because I want to stay in the present
moment for ever, because these present moments are the
only times I'm ever sure of anything. But I'm sobering

up now. I'm coming down from that righteous certainty, and the present moment is in danger of turning into the past. I start to wonder if I can go through with this.

So I do what you always do when the spirit is willing but the flesh is weak: I shut my eyes and think about Jesus when he threw over the moneylenders' tables in the temple, in that passage of the Bible that I read so many times when I was of an impressionable age and getting interested in boys, and in Jesus as the king of boys. I think of that angry and righteous young man in sandals, the son of God taking no bullshit in his father's house, and I channel his rage until there's something there, tingling, pushing me on, making all of this worth it, just for tonight. I was never sure if the rage of Jesus attracted me because I wanted to love him or because I wanted to be him.

And then somehow I get there, and there are noises, and it is Dom, not Jesus, who is murmuring the word 'baby', testing it out in his mouth. How it hangs there in the air. And I'm tired and I don't want to pay my dues by taking him there in return, because this was never really about him anyway. At which point my bedroom door opens and I hear the soft footsteps before I see the small figure. And the small figure turns towards me, opens its mouth and says, 'Mummy?'

PART ONE

Los Angeles

1

In which I accidentally get pregnant

I t had all happened by accident. I hadn't meant to have a baby at all. I hadn't meant *not* to have a baby either, by which I mean I always thought I'd have children one day. It's just that I always thought those children would grow up with me and their yet-to-materialise father in a lovely farmhouse, hugged by the hills, with an Aga and a dog and storybooks and trees and long invigorating walks through the fields in loving drizzle. This was not how I had grown up in Yorkshire but it wasn't a *million* miles from it, either. Several hundred thousand, at a push. It was an idealised version of home, and it lived somewhere vaguely in my future as an unspecified certainty.

Exactly how I thought La Vida Farmhouse was going to appear when I was, in fact, living in a one-bedroom rented apartment in West Hollywood isn't clear. My apartment was just beside the Sunset Strip part of Sunset Boulevard, which is a road that runs for several miles from the Pacific Ocean to the skyscrapers of downtown Los Angeles. The Strip was the glamorously cheesy bit, full of glitzy hotels and rooftop pools and famous people and palm trees, and it was a place that encouraged in me a relationship with reality that could at best be described as negligible. When I wasn't there on the West Side, I was over on the scruffier East Side where most of my friends lived, and on both sides there were parties. Some of them were thrown by my friends, who were lovely people and almost entirely real, and some of them were thrown by the film industry, for people who were paid to pretend to be other people, who were then required to turn up and look like themselves in the photos, which involved a similar amount of pretending. Meanwhile, I felt a strong urge to be honest everywhere and about everything, which is probably why I drank.

I was working as a journalist, interviewing Hollywood celebrities for British newspapers and magazines back home. I had been doing a similar sort of entertainment journalism back in London for several years and now I was here on an American work visa to do it in the heart of the action, the HQ of celebrity itself. It had taken me a good year to ingratiate myself into the Hollywood machine, governed as it was by the sort of publicists who would probably hate me in real life, so it was fortunate that this wasn't real life. I had kissed enough arse and filled enough newspaper pages with writing that was sharp enough to impress but not so sharp as to be offensive. This put me on the right invitation mailing lists, allowed me into preview screenings, and gave me one-on-one access to the preened and the perfected and the shining to try to get them to say things into my Dictaphone that would reveal them to be unravelled and rotten and broken, so that normal people could read about them in the papers and gasp. That was the job. That is still my job today.

One day, my friend Lily had asked me to accompany her across the border to a luxury wellness ranch in Mexico where she would be giving life-coaching lessons, telling lots of rich Californians that all they had to do was follow their dreams and the universe would make those dreams come true (because the universe was structurally biased towards supporting rich white people and their unspoken belief in American exceptionalism – all right, so I can't guarantee that she said these exact words out loud). Lily was a rock in my life, which might seem unlikely, given that she based her life around New Age passions that certain others might describe as 'floaty', 'wafting' or 'woo woo', and given that the only rocks she was interested in were her collection of crystals. These heavy, sharp objects had begun to annoy her downstairs neighbour after she started taking them to bed with her every night, and they rolled off her sleeping body, landing on the hardwood floors with a resounding clunk. This is how you irritate the people in your apartment building in Los Angeles: either with the sound of your crystals going bonk in the night, or your chihuahua yapping incessantly because it isn't getting as much skin-to-skin contact with you as the psychic vet recommended. Or because you've blocked the waste disposal unit after coming home drunk and trying to juice an In-N-Out burger.

Even crystals are not always rocklike in their loyalty: another comrade of Lily's once buried a load of the spiky little buggers in the ground outside her apartment building because she had become convinced they were actively conspiring against her, such was the run of bad luck she'd had since the man in the Purple Moonlight shop in Venice Beach sold them to her. She later dug them up again though, after she went back to the shop to complain that he'd sold her an evil bunch, and he had explained that they weren't taunting her but were, in fact, crying out with a message that her life simply needed to hear. When she recounted this story to me and Lily and I said wow, what an amazing way to get out of giving you a refund, she just stared. So yeah, I wasn't always on the same page as Lily's gang of human moonbeams, but Lil is simultaneously the most loyal, loving, warm, witty human being I've ever met, and our friendship worked. She doesn't ever need a drink, and has never taken a drug because her mind is full of birds floating away already. Speaking of birds, she likes to remind me that all pigeons, all around the world, are called Reg. Apparently, there's a pigeon organisation that has sorted it. Curiously, this has turned out to be true – cast a glance at the next pigeon face you come across and you'll see it. All pigeons *are* called Reg, and there's not a damn thing any one of us can do about it.

So on this ranch in Mexico, all the rich Californians would receive massages from local beauticians, and talk about spirituality and vibes and the universe and say Namaste at the end of all their sentences. Then they would go back to San Diego and Brentwood and Marin County and carry on refurbishing their beautiful houses with the help of Mexican labourers who weren't allowed to use their indoor toilets but instead had to piss in plastic Portaloos because Namaste didn't extend to welcoming the urine of migrant construction workers.

I couldn't afford this retreat, being someone who caught the bus everywhere while living in LA, along with the construction workers. I might have worked among the glamorous but I only earned a few hundred dollars here and there, and was bad at paying bills on time and avoiding fines. I spent all my earnings on bills and fines. In fact, my greatest freelance achievement was the invention of a contemporary dance move that I employed when I needed to stare at the cash machine for long enough to type in the important numbers, but swiftly enough to turn away in a dramatic flourish the moment it flashed up the exact state of my overdraft. But Lily was allowed to bring a partner to the ranch for free, and someone had offered to drive us there in their car, so off we went.

At the ranch, I attended daily power yoga classes run by a breezy, indefatigable woman who made us all feel invincible. Whenever things hurt, she said to work with the pain, go into the pain, feel the pain. It was just as well she said this because I did indeed feel a lot of pain in her class, and on the drive back across the border to LA, after a week of such classes, I felt so much pain that we had to stop at a Mexican service station to beg the universe to give me hardcore pain-relieving drugs. By the time we got back to my apartment in LA, I was feeling so much pain that I was unable to sit down, unable to stand up, unable even to *be*. A day after that I was in the emergency room at Cedars-Sinai hospital in Beverly Hills, which was the place that Paris Hilton and co would end up after paparazzi-induced car crashes, where the Kardashians would give birth, and where Zsa Zsa Gabor would breathe her last before Kanye West arrived having a breakdown. It was, improbably, my local hospital.

It wasn't clear to anyone, including me, quite where this agony was coming from, or if it had anything to do with the exercise at all. It seemed to be in my back, it seemed to be in my belly, it seemed to be in my pee, nothing was clear. I spent a whole day lying on a gurney and being wheeled around to different tests in different parts of the hospital, and having a cash machine wheeled right up to my face by a credit-cardiologist who said that even though I had given them my health insurance details and paid a deposit on arrival, would I like to pay a little something more, just to top it up, before they billed me?

When they said they were sliding me into the big tube for the MRI scan, I felt waves of claustrophobia wash over me. This was worse than the potholing trip we got sent on at school. A man in a lab coat asked me what sort of music I liked, which was even more confusing, until he handed me some big headphones and explained that the music would be piped into my ears during the scan to help me relax. Phew. So they rolled me into that big white tube, and I lay as still as they had strictly instructed

8

me to, and then a voice boomed into my ears. 'Do you want to be STRONG?'

It was the big doomy voice of an American movie announcer. Odd. This was not my music. I mean, yes, I wanted to be strong, hence my being in a hospital. 'Do you want to be ARMY STRONG?' it continued, which, I'll admit, after some reflection, didn't appeal as much. Then, an entire recruitment commercial for the US military followed, and suddenly I could see why the American campaigns in Afghanistan and Iraq had been going so badly for so long. They'd been recruiting their soldiers from hospital beds in Beverly Hills! The only wars we'd win would be against the paparazzi, and even then we'd probably lose. Though, to be fair, my twelve-hour day of hospital testing had also included someone shoving a big cold wand up my vagina and rolling it around like Miss Trunchbull with a rounders bat, so I was feeling quite like starting a battle myself.

Finally, as the evening drew in and after my pain had been toured all around the hospital like a bearded lady in a freak show, they told me that there was good news and bad news. The good news was that the MRI scan had revealed the main problem: I had something like a slipped disc; a vertebra that had come loose from my spinal column and wedged itself forwards into my abdomen while I was busy *feeling the pain* in an exercise class. This sounded like the bad news, but with their Beverly Hills smiles they reassured me it was definitely the good news, as I would not need surgery and it would resolve itself naturally within a week or two if I was sensible and simply became addicted to industrial-strength painkillers instead. Something like that.

The bad news, however, was that while they were poking around up where reality had never been a friend of mine, with Miss Trunchbull's truncheon, they had discovered some trouble in my ovaries, some trouble with some troubling implications. Oh, I know about that, I said, I was already diagnosed as having polycystic ovary syndrome in my twenties, it's not that bad, I've been told it's probably fine. Well, it isn't fine now, they said, it's much worse, and coupled with your hormone levels and your age and— hang on a minute, I thought, *your age*? I was only just into my thirties – all right, I was thirty-four – but nobody had ever said *your age* to me in that tone of voice, suggesting that I had used a lot of my age up already, rather than not had enough of it yet. Regardless, the doctor continued on her merry way, saying that it could still be solved, that I had *the best kind* of infertility, because I could get fertility treatment for PCOS and still carry a child in my own womb. It was just that I would not be able to conceive naturally.

There are times in your life when a whole lot of words collide with each other, serving not just to dredge up your past, but to dredge up your future too. I was more sensitive about my future than I was about my past; I stored more of myself there. In my life, it was as if I was the captain of a magnificent ship but was somehow, always, at this moment, just this one perpetual moment, in a dinghy buffeted about in the ship's wake, always about to catch up with myself. Up ahead on the magnificent ship, I was organised and sober and slim and shiny-haired, all of which was always coming soon, like a trailer in the multiplex that ran in my head twenty-four hours a day. Whatever deadline I was currently missing was always the last deadline I was ever going to miss in my whole life ever, because tomorrow was going to be the perfect day, the most perfect day; the first perfect day of the rest of my perfect life. This infertility news was the first thing to finally break through to me that the ship had sailed off without me this time. For good. That I couldn't keep promising to catch up for ever. Sometimes you miss it and it's actually, truly gone. I went home, shut the door of my apartment and cried for a week.

Obviously, the slipped disc must have contributed to the weeping but I don't remember crying about that; I remember crying because it had finally dawned on me that I had been living in a lovely big pink bubble, a dream world, and that it had burst. I had always got away with leaving things till later, not finishing them, running away and then finding a way to get people to help me pick up the pieces. At school I had never done my homework but never truly suffered any consequences; at university I had crashed in late to every class in my multicoloured rainbow jumper and zebra-skin clogs, starting three separate degrees in three separate years; finishing one just by the skin of my teeth – but it was all right in the end. Now, a lifetime of people making allowances for me was over. What an idiot I had been, thinking that I could go back and make a family later, that I could work out how to have a relationship with a nice man later, just because I thought I was supposed to mess everything up a few times first. Love and sex sat at the two ends of my horizon like feuding siblings who refused to meet. I was nowhere near spawning three children in a farmhouse with a nice man because I didn't know any nice men. What I knew were exciting men, egotistical men, men who ran fast and whom you could sometimes run alongside, as long as you didn't let out a single whisper of genuine need. I was attracted to men who made me think that love was a competition I could win. And then I'd win the competition and turn around and wonder where the love had gone. Men who were humming along to the bassline all the time that I thought we were singing along to the words.

So I sat there with my big bag of industrial painkillers and cried for a week. Until my friend Mal invited me to meet him near his office for lunch, which was a relief, as it required me to wash and dress and look like someone who hadn't been raised round the back of some bins by wolves. Plus, the doctors were right: by the end of the week my spine was fine again. It was just my soul that had changed for ever.

Mal was older than me and widely loved, his career as every creative person in LA's favourite lawyer barely having been dented by the years where he was also his heroin dealer's favourite customer. Now he was just a tennis-playing drunk, so that was all right. We sat in the cafe outside his office and I told him about this most awful diagnosis that I had had, and Mal, a man so laid-back and unflappable that it never made any sense to me that he had needed to take heroin in the first place, listened. At the end of it, when I had finished explaining that this awful news had made me reconsider my whole life and what a fuck-up I had been and how I'd never have the family I wanted, how I had been on this spiritual quest to reconsider my relationship with the world, with my own personal gravity, my gods, my human limitations, how this felt like a great reckoning with me, a great leveller, a moment to take a deep breath and realise what the universe was trying to tell me, that I didn't want fertility treatment, I didn't want chemicals pumped into my body, I wanted a *real relationship*, a family, and that door had slammed shut! Oh, lords above of everything holy, hear my prayer!

Mal sat and listened. And when my monologue ended, he smiled at my lost little face and said, '*Sophie*.' And I said '*Mal*', in that way that you do when you just like to check in with each other's names, make sure you're still there.

'All that the doctors have said to you,' he continued, holding his fork up, grinning slightly, 'is that you can only get pregnant on purpose, not by accident. That's it. That is literally it. Which is, as you would say, *brilliant*.'

An aeroplane flew above our heads towards the airport. I stared and I stared at the words coming out of Mal's face. It was like witnessing God take human form.

'So I think you should celebrate this amazing news,' he continued, 'by going out and fucking like it's the 1970s.'

And that is the story of how I didn't use a condom the next time I had sex, which would turn out to be, as it happened, the very next day (and not, I should add, with Mal, but with someone else entirely), which turned into the story of how I got pregnant and had a baby and became somebody's mother for the rest of our lives, the end. Except it's not the end, is it? Not by a long shot. It never is.

2

All right, the accidental pregnancy actually happens in this one

I remember feeling particularly hot that next night as I left my apartment with Mal's fantastically bad advice re shagging still ringing in my ears from the day before. I remember walking across Sunset and feeling something far beyond the usual Californian heat. It was turning midnight as I made my way there, a fat and juicy moon overhead, cars driving home past me as I walked, the only pedestrian in Los Angeles because I had still not learned how to drive. I remember the bright yellow towelling jacket and black chiffon culottes that I wore, an outfit that I had found in a thrift store in the Valley and been mighty pleased with. I remember how the hotel looked – I remember how all the hotels in Hollywood stirred something in me, the subtle ones, the overpowering ones, the cheap and nasty ones, but how I had chosen my apartment because it was so close to the best: the Chateau Marmont.

This particular hotel had been built as a mock French castle in the slightly ridiculous rococo style that was all the rage in Hollywood in the 1930s, with turrets and pointy sloping roofs and crested balconies, a hazy American impression of old Europe. It was perfect in its sexy wrongness, like a rumour that was so pleased with itself it had decided to come true. Commonly known as the Chateau, it had been a place for Hollywood stars to hide away for decades and showed no signs of stopping. It was dimly lit, with a sitting room full of old dark sofas, lamps, and a grand piano that people sometimes played if the mood took them. I'd been at a few late-night sing-alongs around that lovely thing.

Outside was the garden restaurant with its wicker armchairs and parasols to make people look comfortable while they ever so casually indulged in multi-million-dollar business-deal lunches with actors and directors and other industry types. Or there were couples on dates, or journalists like me conducting discreet interviews. Some of the guests stayed in the rooms upstairs or some paid even more to take up residence in one of the bungalows around the swimming pool – Lindsay Lohan was rumoured to have got stuck living in one for months after the bill grew too high for her to leave.

I was always hanging around there, watching dreams walk past on their own legs. There is something about being that close to people whose dreams actually came true. You're always hoping it's going to rub off on you, or act like an extending dog lead and somehow loop you in, tangle you up in it. Especially since it was so dark in

16

there – even getting into the place involved walking through a corridor so shaded that I would stroll into it in my sunglasses, mid-afternoon, and unfailingly trip on the stairs. I saw David Lynch at the Chateau. Miley Cyrus. Salman Rushdie, Scarlett Johansson, Nicole Richie. Charlie Sheen. Nicole Kidman. Bono grinned at me as we passed on the narrow stairs. I think he thought I was somebody else. I think I did too.

That particular night, though, I remember wondering if I could pass myself off as someone who deserved to be on the inside of that world. I remember trying to walk confidently straight past the hotel reception desk, and then stopping round the next corner to secretly check the text message again. He had told me which room he had arrived in only an hour previously. I just had to find it.

It took me a minute to work out how the rooms in that part of the hotel were arranged, and then I was beside the swimming pool, deserted but still floodlit. That side of the hotel overlooked the pool with an expression of nonchalance, as if it had long since stopped caring how wicked and wild people thought they were being beneath its gaze. I remember hearing a noise and looking up and seeing him, a man I'll call the Musician, grinning down at me. He was waiting for me on his balcony, in a scene that could have come straight out of *Romeo and Juliet*, if it had been set in Los Angeles, and if it had been Juliet who went creeping around at night to find her lover, and if her lover had just flown in from another city where he was playing on tour, and nobody had said 'Wherefore art thou …' but rather, 'Wait, are you dressed as a *bumblebee*?' And if Juliet had looked down at the yellow-and-black outfit she had thought was so coolly different and casually chic, and thought, thundering pissflap arsecakes, I *am* dressed as a bumblebee.

I remember walking round the steps to meet him in his doorway and him already being there to meet me and us not even making it into the room. We were tangled up against the frame; a bee and its sting and the reckless pursuit of honey. Wrapped around each other like we had something to prove, and I suppose we did, even though I would spend many years afterwards wondering what it was, or what would have happened if I hadn't walked up there, or what if that tour hadn't brought him to town, and what if I hadn't injured myself doing *power yoga*, for God's sake, in Mexico?

There was a bottle of whisky on my side of the bed and a bag of weed on his. At the time, I thought how cool it was that we were both wise to our own pleasures. Looking back, I wonder if we were both wise to our own pain. And I took a big gulp of whisky while I laughed and said that we didn't need to use anything, because I definitely couldn't get pregnant, and I swallowed the drink down hard and felt it burn.

The next morning he left for the airport to continue with his American tour. He leaned over and kissed me and told me to stay in bed, get more sleep. I woke up again at noon, realised the cleaners would be coming into the room any minute, and hastily put back on all the clothes that had come off me, retracing them across the room like Hansel and Gretel's trail of breadcrumbs in reverse. Back in the bee costume – well, it had *worked*, hadn't it – I decided to walk a long, winding route home, all around the houses. It was Saturday and I didn't have to do anything, so I strolled along Fairfax, the road that Linda Kasabian had sped Charles Manson down in the getaway car, past Joan Didion's old house. I walked past the Magic Castle, the strange hideaway place, another castle, where you had to be invited by someone in the know to watch magicians do tricks inside hidden walls with disappearing rabbits. I walked past the turning for the 101, the freeway that rolled off towards the Valley and all the big movie studios. The Hollywood sign was up behind me and I still felt the urge to look up at it, to check the hills for something that moved me in ways I couldn't really explain.

And when I got to my apartment, the door of which I never locked, my magical thinking telling me that this made me *more* and not less safe, I walked into the living room, dropped my bag, and sat down at my computer. I didn't have to work, I didn't want to check my email and, for once, I didn't even feel the overwhelming urge to see if people who would bore me senseless in real life had written things either to me or about me in the online one. Just for once, I ignored the internet, and instead I opened a blank document and typed a paragraph that began with these words:

'And one day I will tell you all about how you were conceived in a hotel room in Hollywood.'

My hands seemed to be typing by themselves and they continued for several sentences. I read the whole paragraph

19

back and then a wave of anger rushed over me. I didn't know where the words had come from and they unnerved me. It felt as if something beyond me had written it. I didn't like it. I didn't want Patrick Swayze coming back from the dead to do my pottery for me, thanks all the same. Hadn't I been told, just ten days previously, that I would never conceive a child naturally? Was I taunting myself with a child who had already turned out to be a ghost?

I slammed down the computer lid and got on with my day.

The weeks passed. He and I texted a little. We'd always had a friendship that we dipped in and out of, over many years. We both travelled a lot; the world sometimes washed us up on the same shores. More than anything, we were really good buddies in our own way, and we made each other laugh a lot. I went to see Lily and told her that I had felt, this time, more than any other time, that there was some reason that the Musician and I kept finding each other. I told her how we had lain back on the sofa in his hotel room at one moment and he had said, 'Wait, *how* many years have I known you now?' And how we had done the maths and realised that the one-night stand that first brought us together, in a dressing room some-where in Europe, had now repeated itself, a good number of times, for *seven years*, which had made us both laugh, and then go a bit quiet, wondering to ourselves, that if this wasn't that, that great big love, then what was it? I was trying not to mention the universe because Lily didn't need any bloody encouragement, but dammit, it did feel like there was something there to be said about the – argh.

'Seven years is long enough,' said Lily, matter-of-factly. 'He should put a ring on your finger.'

It was a sweet idea, but felt about as relevant to my life as the idea of learning Swahili or buying a squirrel. Actually, I take that back – I can instantly relate to the idea of learning Swahili or buying a squirrel. But I knew this wasn't a marriage and there would be no ring. In fact, one of the first things the Musician had ever said to me, all those years ago when we met, was that he wasn't the marrying-and-having-children type, and I hadn't said 'Nor am I', even though I had sort of wanted to, because I couldn't decide if it would make me look more or less attractive as a woman, and because there was the La Vida Farmhouse thing, but look, for the most part I just wanted to fool around with him and bitch about famous people and compare notes on the 'Palestinian Chicken' episode of *Curb Your Enthusiasm* while we got wasted. Yet there was *something* that kept bringing us back to each other.

'You should write a book,' he used to tell me. 'You don't really want to be a music critic for ever, do you? It just seems so … limiting for you,' he would say. Nobody else spoke to me like this. They all thought I'd done pretty well to get to where I was, covering music and then film stars for national newspapers. He was the only one telling me to do more, to tell my own bigger stories, and it meant something, coming from him. He was the most amazing person I'd ever met. And so one night after the Hollywood hotel bumblebee and the conversation with Lily it occurred to me that what he had actually given me was a faith in myself I had never had, and so I wrote him a late-night email saying I had realised why the universe had brought us together and it was to encourage me to write a book. And then I went to sleep and woke up in the morning and thought, oh Christ, that isn't right. A week later, he sent a perfectly nice reply saying he was glad to have been some encouragement. And I read it, sitting in my bed and feeling strangely hot again, all over my body, and I thought, nope, it definitely wasn't that at all.

3

What to expect when you weren't expecting to be expecting

Christmas and New Year came and went. My friends went to the desert to take magic mushrooms but I didn't want to go. Mal went away so I stayed in his beautiful house to feed his cat and watch his porn and one night I found a container of ice cream in his freezer. I tasted a bit, sitting on the floor, and when I next held a whole thought in my head it was the realisation that I had eaten the whole carton. I was doing dry January, which publicly I said was because it was good for me, but secretly it was because I had tried a sip of wine and a puff of a cigarette and found I didn't like the taste of them any more, which was so weird that I decided to honour this natural detox window, as Gwyneth Paltrow has possibly never said. By January, I was back in my own apartment on a Saturday night in LA. I knew that something was up because I still didn't want to go out.

But I always wanted to go out. Always. Still, it was probably because I wasn't drinking, I told myself. My period was late, but I didn't keep a particularly close eye on these things. I thought it was due somewhere around now and had a sense that it was time for it to come, but I wouldn't say I carried this information as *factual* knowledge – I just heard it as one of those background hums.

You know how your life can develop a background hum, like a sound that you might hear coming from a fridge or a fan when everything else in the house has fallen still at night? A nagging feeling at the back of your mind that tells you that you have done something foolish which is going to make itself known sooner rather than later but you're going to carry on pretending you haven't? That there's something about to fuck up in the future because you haven't dealt with it? A debt that you didn't pay, which has been multiplying all through your finances, silently. An infidelity that is going to catch up with you. A body that you buried in a shallow grave. Well, it was a Saturday night in Los Angeles and my background hum was getting louder. My whole body was waiting for blood to trickle down my thighs, and it still hadn't come. I was waiting for signs of *no* life. That's what waiting for a period is – waiting for a little death: a *petite mort* of the silent kind.

There were already some clues that something was happening, because I had interviewed the actress Amy Adams a few months before, in a hotel suite at the Four Seasons in Beverly Hills. She was promoting *The Fighter*,

24

a film I had really enjoyed. She told me that when she had first moved to LA she was constantly going to castings and wanting to look pretty. She was broke and had previously worked as a barmaid in Hooters. Then she saw how attractive the woman who served coffee at 6 a.m. in Starbucks was, and she thought, holy fuck, this town – I'm going to need something other than looks. So, she explained, she had worked her arse off on technical skills and humour and timing, and it had got her there instead. I liked her immediately.

She had a one-year-old baby and told me she had truly enjoyed being pregnant. I'd never heard anyone say that before, so I asked her to explain. She said that it was the first time she had felt that her body knew what it was for, that she was so focused, so able to move forward and plough through everything she had to do, her form and her mind united in ambition for once. Something like that. And then, because we are women, trained to need social approval for our every thought, she had politely sought reassurance by saying, 'Do you know what I mean?' and I had replied 'Oh yes, of course!' and I had thought to myself, I have absolutely no idea what Amy Adams is talking about.

Fast forward a few months to January, where I was sober and ploughing through my to-do lists like never before. It had dawned on me that month, sitting at my kitchen table and ticking stuff off, that I was achieving more in one day than I used to in two weeks. It was like I could focus for once, as if my body wanted to move in one direction only, forward, just like – hey – suddenly I remembered what Amy Adams had said, and I knew *exactly* the feeling she had been talking about!

A pink bougainvillea plant was growing all across my window from the yard outside.

Holy fucking shit.

I added these feelings to the hum. Pushed them down. Carried on. Another week passed.

And then it was the Saturday night where I strangely felt no desire to go out at all, and it was time to look back a month in my calendar and work out what inappropriate place I had last been when completely surprised to find I was bleeding into my knickers, because, despite having had this happen once a month since I turned thirteen, it had taken me by surprise every single time.

I counted forward on my fingers. Nine days late. Wow. I might have been an unpunctual sort but nine days seemed a lot. There was a twenty-four-hour drugstore one block down from my apartment. I rolled the thought around in my head for a couple of hours, arguing that it was essential I watch this new Obama speech on CNN and have important and significant thoughts about America as a political entity in a changing world, and find out the latest development in what would become the Arab Spring, and finally, at around midnight, my body put its own shoes on and trudged down to Rite Aid with a ten-dollar bill. It was all I had. My credit cards, debit cards, English and American bank accounts – all were maxed out. In the shop there was a stand with every different kind of pregnancy test, but the cheapest I could see was fifteen dollars. Holy fucking shit again.

And then I saw it: the bargain basement test, the one that didn't have anything complicated with multiple lines or something telling you how many days pregnant you were but instead a very, very simple system. If you were pregnant, the word P R E G N A N T would appear. It cost $9.99 and didn't come with a spare like the others did, so you had to aim your piss right the first time. I bought it, went home, aimed my piss right the first time, and watched the word P R E G N A N T appear.

At 2 a.m. I rang my friend Diane in London, where it was Sunday morning at 10 a.m. This was not a time for texting. 'Do you think,' I asked her, after exchanging literally no pleasantries at all, 'that you could ever be *so* pre-menstrual that all the pre-period hormones in your body are fizzing around so hormonally that they could make a pregnancy test come out as positive when really it means that you're literally about to bleed?'

'You didn't pass biology GCSE, did you?' she replied.

'No,' I said. 'Or chemistry or physics. I went to a shit school and I blame the teachers.'

'Mmm,' she said. 'I don't think pregnancy tests give false positives, only false negatives sometimes.'

'Yeah, but this was the cheapo one so it probably didn't even work.'

'Sophie, they're all the same, you just piss on a stick.'

'Mmm,' I said.

'So, you're pregnant?'

'Mmm,' I said.

And then I went to bed, and as I climbed into it I said out loud, to nobody at all, there is no way I am going to get any sleep tonight, and as soon as my head hit the pillow I slept the entire night through.

4

And when your gynaecologist can't say clitoris

The gynaecologist-obstetrician's practice was in an old-English cottage. Well, that was the official architectural description in the Beverly Hills vernacular, where some fake beams and a rose bush were enough to merit the title, even if the property had been built last Wednesday. Being quite familiar with English cottages, I wasn't used to them being plonked down on large boulevards beside the freeway, full of air conditioning and a waiting room of women who had come to have their vaginas checked. But there I was, to check that the stick I had peed on from the twenty-four-hour drugstore, in fact all three sticks I had now peed on (as I had just been paid for a bunch of articles for *The Times* and could afford more) could not be lying to me. And so the doctor rummaged around inside me, and came out from between my legs again and said no, the sticks were not lying to me, I really was pregnant. The eminently qualified doctor, whose post-graduate certificates lined the walls, confirmed that the baby had been conceived on this one date in the past and was due on this other date in the future, and that I must not consume alcohol or sushi or soft cheese or runny eggs or freebase any crack cocaine, and did I have any questions?

Well, yes, I thought, pulling my knickers back on and wondering if I could ask her if any of this was happening in real life or just in this room, or even just in my head. 'No,' I said out loud, because it was easier, and because I'd just noticed quite how hairy my legs were and was suddenly wondering if this might make the first woman ever to enter this office in Beverly Hills bearing visible traces of our simian ancestry. And because I had spent the last week downloading the entire internet into my brain so there was now nothing I didn't know about early pregnancy. Nothing. Even though it still felt like this condition was merely a delusion of mine and that the gynaecologist was curiously agreeing to support me in the delusion, like some kind of *folie à deux*. Though it did seem curious that someone who had done so many medical courses appeared to be in on the dreaming too.

'Really?' she asked. 'Not one question? Everybody has questions!'

I thought about this. I might have been English but this was America, where you didn't have to be coy. In fact, this was Hollywood, where doctors like her probably implanted wealthy fifty-year-olds with triplets, or fitted coils into porn stars, or dealt with men who wanted to

30

DNA-test their heirs while they were still in the womb, right? And I'd been going to bed with the internet every night that week, scrolling and scrolling through it to find out more and more about the thing that really could not be growing inside me, and there was just one question I hadn't found an answer to. It won't bother her at all. It won't be a thing. I'll just say it. I'll just ask.

'Okay, I do have a question,' I said.

She beamed, brightly. Expectantly.

'Yes. So, is it …' I continued, '… is it safe to use a vibrator?'

She spluttered. The actual medical doctor literally, honestly, spluttered, and if I never knew exactly what spluttering was before, I knew now. And her spluttering set off my automatic response to fill awkward pockets of air with the sound of my own voice, so I heard myself saying, 'Because what it is is, the thing is that the father, the baby's father, he's not in town at the moment, in fact, he's not in the country. In fact, he's not even on this *continent*.'

'*Oh*,' she said. 'Well that does make it difficult,' she nodded, gathering herself. 'I mean, I think what my clients do,' she said, slotting her voice back into its authoritative doctor tone, 'is, when they're pregnant, is, they just use their vibrator on the *front part*.'

Suddenly, there was nothing to worry about any more. I mean, I was probably going to have to give up my job as an entertainment journalist, given that it involved going on tour with bands and attending evening film previews and interviewing actors and directors who constantly changed our agreed times. The baby was going to mess up all of that, and I had no idea how I'd keep my work visa or be able to stay in America, let alone look after a newborn. But now that I knew you could work as a qualified obstetrician-gynaecologist, charging hundreds of dollars to share twenty minutes of your expertise in female sexual health, and still refer to the clitoris as THE FRONT PART, I mean, fuck it – anything seemed possible. I might just work from home as a freelance sayer of the word clitoris. I'd just sit there breastfeeding the baby in my flat and charge people to phone me up so I could say it out loud for them. *Clitoris*. It might even be a nice name for the baby. All right, maybe Clitoria, if it was a girl.

Did I say any of this out loud to the doctor? Of course I did not. What I actually said was 'Oh God, yes, only the front part, yes, that's all I meant, God, ha ha ha!!'

5

In which I break into a house in the Hollywood Hills

My apartment was one of only a handful in a lovely small building, a couple of doors down from Pinches Tacos, a Mexican takeaway where I bought shrimp burritos as often as I could face saying hello to the staff again. (Twice in four hours was my personal record.) Having avoided getting into an extended chat with the burristas, I would creep back to my flat with my spoils, trying to avoid seeing my downstairs neighbours. They were a couple whose dark apartment was filled with mannequins dressed up in theatrical costumes, some of them quite frightening in their preposterousness, and all facing out at the long window to make you do a double-take every time you walked past. And we all had to walk past their long window to get anywhere. So every time you entered the building, you'd jump out of your skin thinking that there were loads of people in sparkling carnival clothes and creepy hats and glasses staring out at you. And just in case you got used to the positioning of the terrifying mannequins, the couple would move them in the night, ready to surprise us afresh in the morning.

The couple didn't speak to anyone else in the building. I'm not entirely convinced they even spoke to each other. They were both bronzed, with pumped-up muscles, their faces always looking as if they were about to burst. The landlords had allegedly been longing to get rid of them for years but there was rent control and they had tenants' rights.

Over time, I would learn that every apartment building in Hollywood, whether small like ours (only six apartments) or containing a whole village, had people very like this, people I would have been fascinated by had I not had to share a washing machine with them. People who'd come to Hollywood to do something or other in the industry, but the sun or the drugs or the abuse of power had got to them and now they shared their life with a carer, or a little dog with a leg missing, or a pet turtle who would periodically escape from their yard in search of a plot development. Their orange faces were smoothed out by Botox and enough resentment to fuel a factory. They were everywhere, the walking wounded of Hollywood, with just about enough money to live on, queuing up at Ralphs and Trader Joe's with discount vouchers, wearing Hawaiian shirts and ironed smiles and painted rage.

You didn't call it Hollywood though, you called it 'the industry' and everybody knew what you were talking about. At parties, people would ask if I worked in the industry, which was a straightforward question, although over time I had changed my answer. It had started off as, 'No no, I'm from England, I'm a journalist for newspapers in London.' Gradually, I had realised that, given that I interviewed actors and directors about their shows and films and I did this within the industry, that yes, I too worked in the industry, just like the dog walkers and the make-up artists and the drivers, the valets and cleaners and builders. We were all making it in 'the industry' somehow. But I didn't want to stay down in the dusty apartments. I wanted to make it up into the houses, into the hills.

I lacked the fixed income with which to do this, but the distance between dreams and reality had never been wide apart enough to stop me obsessing over impossible things for at least a quarter of my day, every day. I signed up to a mailing list of properties for sale, and I'd some-times look up the address and walk up into the hills and stare at them. At the weekends, there were open houses where you could dress up all smart and pretend you were interested in buying the place, and the agent would show you and a bunch of other random strangers around the rooms while you nodded approvingly in all the right places and then scarpered before they noticed that your car was not parked where they had told you to park it, because you didn't actually have one, and that your armpits were sweating from your pedestrian ascent of the hill.

Unfortunately, these open houses were typically held in the more ostentatious properties that had been stripped of any character they may once have had and turned into glass and aluminium and marble McMansions. I was nosy about them, sure, especially if Kanye West had once owned it (there seemed to be about a one in ten chance of this.) But the houses I loved were the scruffier, artsier ones that were still holding strong against the yuppification of the hills. These canyons had a strong boho history and it was those 'character properties' I dreamed of. Which was no more realistic – they cost millions too.

Some pregnant people go to antenatal yoga classes as their chosen form of exercise. I similarly believed, in those early days, that it was very important for me to stay physically active and fit in my gestation, which is why I continued with my sweaty walks into the hills to stand outside total strangers' houses and stare at them for as long as I could before security came out to have a word with me. So one day, when I got a notification on my phone about a house that had just come onto the market, I decided to go and have a look. There was a photo included of a room with huge paintings hanging on the walls as if the artist had just painted them and they might still be wet. As it happened, I was in Mal's car, coming back from a Sunday brunch in Griffith Park with a few of our friends. He was giving me a lift home when I told him, suddenly, to drop me somewhere else, and being a smooth sort he didn't ask why, so he took me there and carried on his way. There I was, outside the property that felt, to me, like it was already mine, especially as there was a whole artist's studio inside it.

The house was built into the hillside, so the living space and art studio were upstairs and the bedrooms were mainly on the lower level. I had always loved those upside-down hillside houses; it was definitely mine. The house was set back from the road with a decent sized lawn in front, so I walked up the path and peered in some windows. Not much going on in there. It looked lived in, yes, but quiet. It seemed like nobody was home. I walked up the steps that ran up beside the house, gripping the hill. I peered in more windows; nothing much going on in there. I got to the back and I felt my reckless streak whooping inside me, telling me to test the doors. They were all locked, except for one, which opened in my hand just like the recklessness said it would. Look, this door into the kitchen is unlocked, said my bad conscience. Give it a knock. Wait without breathing. See, nobody's there. Because it's yours. You're allowed this. Could be yours. Might as well be yours. Will be soon enough, anyway.

So I walked right in, through the kitchen, through the living room, until I found the art studio, which was double the height of the other rooms and spectacular. I waited to see if anybody would appear, but nobody did. I had a pee in the toilet. I sat outside on the balcony, which had a sofa on it, overlooking the street. I stared at the art and went back to the kitchen, which was full of food and signs of family life. There were no letters on the mat, though, which made it hard to work out the names of the people who lived there. So I went through a stash of papers on their kitchen shelves until I found an engagement diary that had the owner's full name on it. I wrote it down on my phone, as if it was a clue. I read the diary for a while. About half an hour passed, maybe more. It was nice in my new home.

At some point I left, and walked all the way back to my apartment, thinking, yes, I can do this, I can have this baby in Los Angeles, look at the way we live here! There was no need to return to my native England because my nesting instinct had clearly kicked in. This baby and I were going to be just fine.

6

In which I tell him

Well, you know what's coming now. I have to tell him. I have to summon up all of the strength inside me to break it to the Musician that he's going to be a father. And I don't know if we're starting a family or starting a war. My best news – and it is, truly, starting to feel like my best news, like it all makes magical sense somehow – could be his worst. The truly terrifying thing about it is that I have to tell him over the phone, in my speaking voice, because sending a text saying 'we're having a baby' seems a little informal, even by my standards. I'm not sure I've actually phoned someone up to have an important conversation with them in about five years, not since they made phones so sickeningly brilliant that you never want to talk into one of them again.

So I did it. He was thousands of miles away and not expecting to hear from me. In fact, I talked so fast when he answered that he couldn't hear what I said, and asked me to repeat myself, which meant I had to take a deep breath and deliver my big news all over again. I hadn't banked on having to say it *twice*, though as a writer I suppose it was nice to get a chance to edit my words and work on the sentence structure in real time. His response didn't improve, though – I later realised it wasn't that he hadn't heard me, but that he hadn't been able to process the words that were coming out of my mouth, because they were impossible. And so these phone conversations continued, over the weeks, turning into a big old argument: disbelief, terror, and sometimes tenderness too. And every time, I would put my hands to my belly, where barely anything existed beyond a particle theory of cells. My womb had been nothing but a private joke between me and the gods at this point but I worshipped it all the same. I knew the miraculous accident was here to stay.

People ask when I decided to keep the baby, but it wasn't a decision. There was never anything to decide about that. This baby felt as real to me as the North Star from the minute I read the word on the drugstore stick. It was made of both bone and metaphor. It was allegorical. It was literal. It was figurative. It was sprouting inside me. I had grown up in a cerebral, bookish family where we pushed our brains to think harder, and oh, what pure pleasure there was in this unthinking state. Pure physicality – I felt as if I was becoming a cow, as if pregnancy had given me the gift of cow-ness. I chewed my cud, adapted to my bovine condition, and argued with someone who was not feeling the wild like I was, someone who feared this monstrous growth, this unanticipated snatcher of our lives as we had known them. He said a child deserved better than us, and was terrified that we couldn't create the stability that a whole new person deserved. We entered into philosophical disagreements about a material thing. Or were they material disagreements about a philosophical thing? It's particularly hard to tell when you still fit into your jeans.

A friend I barely knew was in town from London. The usual thing to do with a visitor from London at night was to drink until I had shaken them from the notion of going to Hollywood Boulevard and trying to make friends with the guy who walked along it dressed as Jesus, but I couldn't drink, so I had to tell this fairly random friend that I was pregnant. He was very nice about it and said we should go to the cinema, so we slunk into some seats near the front to watch whatever was on. It turned out to be a film in which Michelle Williams grew more stressed and Ryan Gosling grew more drunk. Oh, it turned out to be a bad choice – in this story, she got pregnant and went to a clinic to have the abortion, having agreed that this baby was impossible, that they couldn't do it, they were just young fools, irresponsible, no future to offer a child. But then, lying there in her white medical gown, ready for the procedure, she bolted. She couldn't go through with the abortion and ran out still in her gown. I knew then, without a shadow of a doubt, that I was her, and that that would be me if I ever got as far as making it through the front gates of a clinic. This baby might be impossible but an abortion was only more so, as illogical to me as getting on a spaceship or cutting my hand off and then saying in years to come, hey, that was a really good thing I did back there for my arm. I had been through abortions with friends, going with them to the hospital or clinic to keep them company. I had once even watched the full operation happen, as this particular friend was living in a country where it was all done in front of you, with the medics very blasé about it, and I had flown out to look after her and hold her hand all the way through it. I would have done it again tomorrow for any friend who needed it. But that didn't mean I could do it myself.

The film travelled forward five years, and there they were again, their marriage now having become impossible. She was the responsible parent who earned the money and got their little girl to school on time, and there was Ryan Gosling, who only wanted to drink and play endless games where anything could be anything and time didn't matter, and then drink more. The magical, selfish, pissed arsehole. And then I knew that I was him.

That same week, I had spent hours in my local bookshop on Sunset Boulevard, nervously scanning the shelves for a guide to show me the way through the situation I found myself in. All I could find were books called things like *What To Expect When You're Expecting*, full of advice on folic acid and obstetricians and when to decorate the nursery and how your husband should give you a back rub to ease the tension of growing another person inside your person. I couldn't look at these books for very long. They made my back feel cold.

What I longed for was to find a book called *What To Expect When You Weren't Even Fucking Expecting To Be Expecting*, which would tell you what to do when you found yourself standing on Santa Monica Pier holding your phone in your trembling hand, desperate to hurl it into the Pacific Ocean so the thoughts of a scared and angry man couldn't buzz through it any more; so you would be free of other people's opinions on whether this unexpected item should be inside your bagging area at all. He still thought there was a chance to change my mind; I still thought there was a chance to change his. We had to stay in regular communication, and sometimes it could be sweet, even, on a very good day, to the point of us discussing potential baby names that we liked. We weren't going to become a couple, but there were moments where we could be friends, partners in some crazy new adventure, almost laughing about it. But mostly we were at war and it was grim.

I didn't want to read about folic acid, I wanted to read about what happens if you're a person who used to take party acid and even though it's been fifteen years since then, there's a part of your brain that will for ever be somewhere in a field, and you want to phone your mother and say, Mother, something has happened and I can never come home again – but now you're about to be the person on the other end of the phone, the one called Mother – and – how the hell does *that* work out?

I wanted to find a pregnancy book that told me how to breathe for two when I wasn't sure how to breathe for one, and if I would really be able to look after this child when I wasn't entirely sure I could look after myself. I wanted a book that would tell me how to prepare my child for life with only one parent, but a book that also explained that yes, that surge you're feeling deep inside is not heartburn and it's not hormones: it is joy. It is actual *joy*. Because I felt joy all right.

I walked home from Book Soup, along Sunset Boulevard back to my apartment, when a scruffy blond guy who looked like he was high on crack started walking towards me, staring right at me like maybe he was going to rob me. Normally I would have tightened my grip on my handbag. But this time my hands went straight to my stomach, my womb, before any thought or recognition of the situation even entered my head. In fact, my head seemed to have nothing to do with it. Pure instinct. I knew then that, without a shadow of a doubt, I was going to have this baby, and that I could trust in my physical form to take over. My cow-ness was also my wolf-ness. Sharpened claws, with which to protect my young. That was the moment I became an animal.

I was walking down Melrose Avenue. There is no point in ever beginning a Los Angeles anecdote with 'it was a sunny day' and yet I feel duty bound, sitting here in East London in the winter as I type this, to point out that it was a sunny day as I walked down Melrose, a street known for its noisy fashion boutiques and mid-century modern furniture shops. And then I saw it, in the window of the Vivienne Westwood store, which I had never entered. I knew all about Westwood and loved the idea of her, but her clothes had always been out of my league. Then I saw a dress by her in the window, not one of her fitted, sexy ones, as they might have been hard to fit around a bump that was enlarging by the day. No, this was a big, loose grey T-shirt dress, not Vivienne Westwood's usual style at all except for the enormous red, gold and black snake winding its way all over it, challenging anyone who looked at it.

Me and that snake stared at each other, its big pouting red tongue hissing out, and I knew. I went inside. It cost $400. It was the stupidest thing I could possibly do, at a time of financial insecurity, not knowing what my future held. Nobody in their right mind, when pregnant, adds $400 to their credit card debt for what is essentially a T-shirt. But it seemed a small price to pay for a body-guard. I took it home and put it on and I barely took it off again. I wore it the day I gave birth. There is a photo of me standing on the roof of Homerton Hospital, East London, having tried to speed up my contractions by climbing up a fire escape, protected by that beast of a dress.

Back at my LA apartment, there was nothing I wanted to eat or at least could face cooking. It was a Tuesday and I was alone and I suddenly couldn't be alone, or cook for myself, or do the work of the caring person as well as the person in need of care. So I went across the road to the Chateau. I got a table in the posh restaurant bit. Not the usual living room area, where I would sometimes sit in the afternoons and eke out one pot of tea for four hours, or the outdoors bit where famous people picked at the protein in their carbless salads, but the little dining room with the muted lights and sexily austere vibes. I sat alone at a dark wood table like a character in a horror film who has just murdered every member of her family, and I ordered the $25 spaghetti Bolognese, the staple food of my childhood, the taste of home. I thought it would feel like being loved. I sat and ate it and it felt nothing like it whatsoever.

7

In which I tell them

I wanted to tell my family. I was close to my family. Possibly too close, which is why I was also really enjoying living on the other side of the world from them. My mum, a social worker, had the sort of piercing observational skills that would have given her any job at MI5 that she wanted, and it had been quite refreshing to live one step removed from this, with only the Santa Ana winds going down my neck, rather than her breath.

'I've been looking at a floorplan of your flat,' she used to say, back when we lived in the same country, 'and there should be a four-inch gap between your boiler and the external wall. So you should move your ironing board there.' Off I would trot and discover that, lo and behold, the perfect spot for my ironing board indeed existed, there inside my flat in Bethnal Green, detected from her home in Yorkshire, all this time. Or I would mention that I'd seen a friend that day, a friend my mother didn't know, only for her to then recite their whole name and reveal she'd found some online evidence of me meeting them already, and sent them a message about it, and expressed her surprise that we'd had to travel to our destination in a *taxi*.

I couldn't even blame her for following my life like a reality TV show – I grew up in a Yorkshire village so boring that if you were seen eating more than two eggs, somebody would jump up and warn you that you were soon to become 'egg-bound'. It's not surprising that I wanted more, a feeling that led me to move away from the north of England to London, and then culminated in me moving from England to Los Angeles, the most exciting place of all, where eating more than the white part of an egg would lead somebody to jump up and warn you that you were soon to have elevated cholesterol levels. Oh.

A village near York was a wonderful place to grow up, but you do have to consider the sacking and burning of the region by Ivar the Boneless. Now, I'm not saying that people referred to this particular Viking conquest on a *daily* basis, but there was something in the air. I actually don't believe the Vikings ever left York – they just started dressing in plain clothes. The Romans may have come and gone, and the Tudors and the others all had their turn on the historic fairground that is the fair city of Eboracum, Jorvik and whatever other name it's been known by in its long and memorable existence – but it's the Vikings who you still feel lurking around you, waiting to get a good look through your bins. Who mercilessly pillage your outfit with their eyes and then ask you, slyly, 'What have you come as?', the joke being that your fashionable clothes suggest you have mistaken everyday life for a fancy-dress party.

I was always told that the farming village I grew up in, Ulleskelf, took its name from a Viking chieftain called Ulle. Though some years had passed since his demise – over a thousand, in fact – it appeared still to be under the rule of the Danelaw and, even though the Treaty of Alfred and Guthrum had been formalised in 886, my primary school considered me a suspicious foreigner, because my parents were both southerners, and a bit posh. My mother had first aroused local suspicion by breastfeeding, which was seen as a perverted thing to do when formula milk was freely available at the Co-op, and had then made it even worse for herself by really enjoying going to work. 'Ooh, it'll be so nice for you to be off your feet and have a rest,' said the lady next door when my mum got a broken sewing needle stuck in her foot, went to hospital with suspected blood poisoning, and was signed off on crutches for eight weeks. Given that Mum had once attended a coffee morning for local women and found herself, after the which-brand-of-sunglasses-do-you-wear chat entered its fortieth minute, praying for the sweet release of death, the thought of eight weeks off work did her far more damage than the eye of the needle that had been making its way towards her veins. We weren't village people; we were people who lived in a village.

But no, there was no point in me trying to gain any privacy from my mother, and God knows I had tried. I deleted her from my Facebook once and I can't remember exactly how she got back on there, but I imagine a call to Mark Zuckerberg's home landline was involved. Or maybe she got Cambridge Analytica to do it. I mean, she

49

definitely works for them. Or she should, as it would make their job so much easier. Data on 30 million individuals can be accessed via my mother's own brain for free.

She once had to go and speak to a select committee in the Houses of Parliament about a social work matter, which was very exciting, and I can imagine that she was brilliant, having spent years dedicating herself to child protection and social policy issues. Afterwards, she read up the transcription of the discussion in Hansard, and realised that the publication that had transcribed everything said out loud in the House of Commons for over a hundred years had misquoted her. So she rang them up, and managed to get put through to the man who had done the typing.

'Mrs Heawood,' he insisted, presumably with the voice of someone who had been doing this job for some time, flawlessly, *relentlessly*, 'the meeting was recorded and we annotated everything exactly as it was said. You have not been misquoted.' But this thing you've written here about X, she said – that's not what I said. He insisted that it was indeed exactly what she said. It must be. It had to be. 'Well, all right, it might be what I *said*,' she continued, undeterred, 'but it isn't what I *meant*. So you'll have to change it.'

I have discovered, over my lifetime, that there is simply no point trying to argue with someone who tries to argue with Hansard.

My father, meanwhile, is a retired philosophy lecturer, sixteen years my mum's senior. Not quite so clued-up on the minutiae of my life, yet closer to the material in more organic ways, since he and I seem to share the same brain. I know every one of his stories by heart, know my way around his thought processes with my eyes shut, and always know which bit of the television programme he is going to shout at. I feel nothing but comfort when he says things like, 'Of course the translator I supplanted when I took the job for the Pentagon was a young Japanese man who had defected to the USA after having an affair with the wife of an admiral', before he adds that the admiral 'had *presumably* fixed his immigration papers to get rid of him'.

(This story is misleading. He actually got a job at the Pentagon in the 1950s because he'd been working on an oil rig in Canada, came to America and joined a temping agency, who promptly asked him if he could speak French. No, he replied, which turned out to be a shame as they needed someone to translate material for a government military handbook about Papua New Guinea into English. Some weeks later, they asked him again if he could speak French. Yes! he replied this time, and got the job. Something I find hard to imagine, given that he went on to spend the rest of his life as a peace activist.)

Still, it would be all right, I told myself, because I had the sort of relationship with my parents where I could have long conversations with them about absolutely anything: sex, love, grief, ecstasy, existential angst. As long as I was talking about somebody else's life, and not my own. My brother, meanwhile, was the opposite of me, the one who was good at sitting in libraries and studying all day, the one who had got into Cambridge, the one who had got married at twenty-nine and had a family. Which is why it did not entirely fill me with elation to ring any of these fuckers up and say, hey, guess what your hot mess of a daughter/sister has done *now*? Still, the main thing was that I needed to tell both my mother and father at the same time, as they insisted on being involved in things together, and then I could ring my brother after that.

This plan was, of course, foiled when I rang my parents' number on a Friday evening, their time, only to find out that my mum wasn't there. It was just my dad on his own, as she'd gone to stay with my brother and his family in London. Aargh. I couldn't tell him without her, but I also couldn't ring her in London and tell everyone there without my dad. It would have to wait. My dad asked if there was anything he could help with and I said, er no, was just going to have a chat with Mum, at which he asked why I didn't ring her in London, at which I said, yes, maybe. Only for me to try their Yorkshire number again two days later, only for him to tell me that she *still* wasn't back. Dammit. 'Is everything all right?' he asked, and I said, yes, absolutely, of course, Daddy, no problemo at all!

By the time I got them both together I'd been dying to tell them for days, so I told them, and my mum said to me, 'You know, this might not be the right man, and it might not be the right time, but it's the right baby', which I thought was the sweetest thing anybody had ever said to anybody else in the whole world, and which gave me a lump in my throat and filled my heart with gladness.

Until my mother revealed that she had nicked the line from a *Sunday Times* interview with pop star Sophie Ellis-Bextor and her mother Janet Ellis. My mum then explained she'd had time to practise the line before repeating it to me, because my dad had already told her that I was pregnant.

But *how*, I said, *how* did Daddy know?

'Well, he didn't actually know for sure, but we knew that something was going on because you kept ringing us up and not asking for any money,' she replied.

Oh, I said.

8

Meanwhile, my best friend is inserting an egg into herself

So I'm sitting in a cafe with Lily and eating a shrimp burrito. There was a period when I had been eating kale salads for lunch, like a real Angeleno, but it turned out it was the kale salads that had got me pregnant. Now that I'm reading long sections of pregnancy guides while on my knees in bookshops (they're all so annoying that I'm not willing to pay for them, only scour their content for free, and why they always put them on such low shelves is beyond me, almost literally) I've discovered that kale is a fertility superfood you're supposed to eat if you want to boost your chances of conceiving. And now I'm annoyed, because I genuinely had no idea. They should have come with a warning. Some kind of provisory notice saying Please Be Warned That If You Eat This Every Day For Six Months And Then Have Rampant Unprotected Sex With A Man While Ovulating You Could Get Knocked Up.

And Lily says, how's that thing that's growing inside you, and I say, apparently, it is the size of a tennis ball, and she says, it's a bit of a bummer that you have to go through all of this to give birth to a tennis ball, and I say, easier on the perineum though, and she says, ooh, guess what I'm doing this weekend? And I say, something involving the perineum? Yes! she says, which I'll admit is not what I was expecting. Lily isn't as bothered about sex as I am. She tends to prefer thoughtfulness to shagging.

I'm going to a group-sharing circle about female masturbation, she says. It's in Mount Washington. We have to bring an egg.

An egg? I say.

Not a chicken egg, she says. A yoni egg. For the guided group activity.

Oh my God, I say. You mean you're all going to put one of those freezing cold jade things up your fannies and then sit round in a circle reaching climax together? I say.

It's a non-climactic circle, says Lily, sounding very well informed about it. I'm about to laugh at the thought that there could also be climactic ones but I manage to suppress it.

There are also climactic ones, says Lily.

Wow, I say.

We sit there.

Well, ask me what I'm doing this weekend, I say.

What are you doing this weekend, she says.

Trying to get an egg *out* of my yoni, I say. Wait, no, I have more questions, I say, how did you find out about this wanking group? Is it a secret?

I've been on a waiting list to join, she says.

You were on a waiting list to join a *wank bank* and you never told me?

Yes, it's amazing I held it back, given how well you've reacted, she says.

No no, I *love* it, I want to come too, I say.

It's too late for you, she says. Your egg's already fertilised. Your goose is cooked.

So I tell Lily that I actually had the best self-loving experience the other day. That I had been going to tell her all about how pregnancy affected masturbation, how I hadn't known that this was a side effect, like when all the blood rushes to a penis and causes the erection and—

Actually, the clitoris *is* as big as a penis, interrupts Lily, and it's a myth that women have to choose between vaginal or clitoral orgasms because the clitoris is in fact this one great iceberg type thing that goes all the way through. It's huge.

Anyway, I continue explaining, I had realised that, clearly, this new weight upon my genitals had been pushing down and making me super sensitive. It was so easy to make myself come, I couldn't believe it. It took, like, seconds. The whole area was tingling like it was on *fire*.

Wow, she says.

Yeah, I say. Except I had a doctor's appointment the next day and when she looked she told me I had a bacterial infection and she gave me these really fast-acting antibiotics and now my vagina feels completely normal again when I touch it. It wasn't on fire. It was thrush.

Oh, she says.

Oh Sophie, she adds.

Then I ask Lily how she first got onto this waiting list and she says she heard about it in the crystal shop, and I ask her whether that would be the same crystal shop where her friend bought the bad juju ones that she had to bury and dig up again because the handsome salesman said she wasn't *hearing their message.*

That's not it! she protests, you've got it quite wrong.

All right, what did he actually say to her?

He said that she had *misinterpreted their data.*

And that's why she drove home and exhumed them again?

It was a learning experience, replies Lily.

For who? I say.

For the crystals, she replies, and I just can't tell if she's joking.

9

And now I'm trying to come out to Jodie Foster

I f there's one thing worse than having morning sickness and not being able to tell anyone because you're newly pregnant with a baby that nobody knows you are having, it's having morning sickness and not being able to tell anyone because you're newly pregnant with a baby that nobody knows you are having, while simultaneously walking the wrong way down an American freeway that runs through a cliff and has no pavement, with cars whizzing past you at eighty miles an hour as you creep along the road itself, because you came to Bel Air on a creaking public transit bus because you can't drive, and because the bus only stops in a few random places so you got off in one that seemed near enough to your destination, and you perhaps miscalculated and then took a wrong turn on to this road but you just have to keep walking now, because when you get to the destination, which is a luxury hotel, you're going to interview Jodie Foster, starting in ten minutes' time, and it will look bad if you interview Jodie Foster in a luxury hotel with vomit all down your top, and it will look even worse if you're dead.

As a child, when not in one of my lengthy conversations with God or the voice of an imaginary bear, I was often to be found watching *Bugsy Malone*. My brother and I couldn't believe that the entire cast of this amazing musical set in Prohibition-era America were children. Jodie Foster played Tallulah, who sang in the speakeasy and drove men wild with desire for her. It was my first experience of a femme fatale, and I was obsessed, her eyes narrowing with kohl and coolness as she sang about forgetting men's names.

The men of *Bugsy Malone* drove around in rattly buggy cars and fired custard pies at each other out of splurge guns, while Tallulah remained back at the speakeasy, with a certain stillness to her. Even when she sang and danced her way around the men, her head barely seemed to move, her eyes barely registering the interruption to her distant gaze. She was alluring. She was a cat. She was the cream. She was the stillness that they had to move towards. I watched it again and again, pausing the VHS tape that we had recorded off the telly so I could write down the words to all the songs and learn them by heart.

I wanted to sing like her but I wasn't sure I wanted to be her, or that I *could* be her, with the way she narrowed those sexy cat eyes, and the sheer confidence she had in the demands that she made. To be quite honest, I identified more with the splurge guns, and it is fair to say that

I have lived most of my life since then less as a femme fatale and more as a custard pie, mid-flight, looking to land on a golf buggy.

The Tallulah love had remained strong though, somehow only strengthened by the discovery that Jodie Foster was probably a lesbian. To think that the person who, aged thirteen, had the capacity to win the competition for men (and I always saw it as a competition, though not against other women, but against the men themselves) didn't actually *want to enter it*. It was a huge relief to me, somehow.

So, several decades after she played that part, here I am, making it off the tarmac and up into the hotel in the nick of time. My nerves are rattling around my chest like a bag of lightbulbs. There are surfers not far from here, standing on the beach just half a mile away and waiting for the Pacific to provide them with the perfect wave. If only they knew that the waves are all to be found in my stomach, which is currently churning like an ocean swell. I can do this, I say to myself, and then also, every few minutes, I can't do this, because my inner voice is also going to be sick.

I get to the correct room after asking at the front desk, and once a publicist has ushered me in and sat me down I am taken aback by how nice Jodie Foster is. She is so nice. She's a rock-solid presence, grittily determined to see the good in things. She gives off a vibe of love, but the hard-earned type – a love not given but created, worked-on, figured out, puzzled over and come out the other side of, to love again and love more. The interview is for a glossy psychology magazine, so we get stuck in to the meaty questions of life itself: how she has made peace with it all in her head on the cusp of turning fifty.

Of course, there is one rule about interviewing Jodie Foster, and it's not a rule that anyone expressly spells out to you beforehand, but it's one that everyone in the industry knows. And it is that, while everyone is pretty sure she's gay, and that she has had two children in a relationship with her long-term lesbian partner, which is now thought to have ended, she has never spoken about her love life publicly. She's not out. She won't tell you anything. And she's a legend and you have to respect her privacy, because she surely has her reasons and is entitled to her reasons, and outing people isn't cool or necessarily even helpful to the gay cause, because who are you to make marginalised groups perform for you?

Which is fine by me, because I've already realised that it's me who actually wants to come out to her. Jodie, I want to say, *listen*, you've been through a thing or two, Jodie, I'm *pregnant* and I haven't told anyone yet, you're a single mother, you're the only person I can talk to about this, Jodie – what the hell am I going to do?

I'm desperate to tell her. The words are bubbling over inside my mouth, along with the feeling of sick about to come out.

She tells me that she has just realised that all the films she has made herself, now that she's a director, are about spiritual crisis; people trying to choose between their head and their heart.

I nod, agreeing so hard, trying not to be sick.

'Spiritual crises are these little things,' says Jodie Foster to me in hushed, intimate tones, 'a moment in time where you believe you have to choose between life and death.'

I nod again, agreeing so hard, still trying not to be sick.

I ask the famously private woman about her kids.

She tells me that parenting is her most artistic act, that you're part of watching this thing blossom that is outside you and yet part of you, the best part of you.

I nod again, terrified, excited, my most artistic act, the best part of me, trying not to be sick.

We discuss how she was raised in a single-parent family and became a child actor at the age of three, making her into the breadwinner. Three!

She says she believes she was born to carry that burden, apologising for how New Age Californian that sounds.

I nod again, still trying not to be sick, willing to take all the Californianisms anyone has got. I've spent the past week reading runes in places where there are no runes. I've tried to talk to my dead grandmother. I've prayed. I've been to see a fortune teller in Beverly Hills who told me that things were going to get better for me sooner than I thought. Since then, things have only got worse.

Jodie Foster tells me that life presents a whole new set of challenges in middle age, especially now that people are having kids much later.

'I have small children,' she says, 'I have an ageing mom, those are my two big ones and ...' she falters, 'and ... in *other people's lives* they have divorces.'

I realise she is trying not to tell me about the end of her long relationship with her last girlfriend, while also trying to tell me about it. She says something else about the terrible things that happen in family life, something about death and divorce and disintegration, and something about freedom, how you also have ten seconds in those tough moments to grab your freedom, your own life, a sliver of opportunity. In hindsight, I think her long-term relationship had ended and perhaps another had already begun, right there. I think she was speaking like someone in love. But that wasn't really on my mind, because before I know it, it all shoots out of my mouth, right there, into the room, in front of her.

Not vomit. And not my big secret. No, what shoots out of my mouth is the question of whether she is going to *come out*. Oh, Christ alive, I've only gone and done it. I've asked Jodie Foster if she's a lesbian. This is a Hollywood no-no.

And she grins. This may be an extremely sophisticated technique of psychological disassociation from a difficult confrontation but I ask Jodie Foster about being gay and she motherfucking grins.

'I've never come out to anyone,' she says, and then she grins again and adds the words '*publicly*, at least.'

Oh my God. Those words are enough.

She then tells me, in a very warm way, that I am to think what I want to think, and to write what I want to write.

So that's it.

As far as I know, she has never said even this much to a journalist before. Jodie Foster has been in the public eye for forty-seven years, somehow maintaining all her

63

privacy throughout, and now I've almost accidentally got the scoop. There's only one thing that makes a journalist more nervous than not getting the scoop and that's *getting* the scoop. Fuck. My nerves are falling through my bones.

It is time to leave so I pick up my Dictaphone and my notes and my handbag and say my polite goodbyes and shut the hotel suite door behind me. I walk down the corridor to get out of this hotel and think to myself that maybe, just maybe, I might be allowed to treat myself to a taxi home, if the alternative is rolling into the ocean and plunging into the sea. Which feels entirely possible right now. I'm on the very edge of America; I'm on the very edge of my life.

'HEY, EXCUSE ME,' shouts a voice, bringing me back to reality. By this point I am halfway down the long luxurious corridor, which is painted in various shades of money, and who is this person shouting at me? I turn around to find that I am being pursued by a Hollywood publicist wearing a tight skirt and heels. Her job is to ensure that nobody ever speaks their mind or says what they mean or enjoys their life in any meaningful way.

She reaches me.

'So, like, some of that stuff that was said in there I think wasn't relevant to the movie, and I think we just need to check you're not going to use all of it in this piece?'

I didn't even know this woman had been listening to the interview. I knew she'd been in the room at the start but when she disappeared from sight I naively thought she'd left, not just gone round the corner into an adjacent part of the suite to eavesdrop. When will I learn that

Hollywood trusts nobody? Now she's speaking in code and I know exactly what she means, which is that I'm not allowed to print the conversation we just had about Jodie's sexuality.

'I'm not sure what I'm going to use yet,' I reply, 'but the Dictaphone was clearly on and Jodie chose to speak into it.'

'Yes, but,' the publicist carries on, being all fake nice and pally with me and how isn't it in the best interests of everyone if blah and bleurgh and I don't even remember what she says after that. Something about how I've broken the rules of some interview deal I agreed to promising that I would stay on topic. Maybe I even signed a document. I think I did sign a document. I feel even more sick.

She says once again that I can't use that material and I say well we'll have to see when I write it up, no decisions being made right here right now. I somehow get away from the woman.

Two days later, after an email battle between various people – the publicist, her bosses, my bosses, me – I surrender. I've been working my arse off to build a career here in Hollywood for a couple of years now, and I'm too anxious and vulnerable to burn any bridges right now. These publicists all represent several big-name stars each, and if they blacklist you and pass your name on to other publicists to blacklist, they can make it very hard for you to work as a journalist in Hollywood. Your editors will become unable to give you any work because your access to the celebrities will be revoked. And as a freelancer with no salary, no maternity pay, on the verge of becoming a single mother, it's just too scary to contemplate. So I agree not to print it while fuming inside about the fact a wonderful woman who seems to have love in her life is somehow bad. It's disgusting. All these little dark secrets – whose darkness is it? All of our secrets, all of them sprung from love.

Three years later, I am sitting in Hackney, East London, in some cafe or other, nursing a cold cup of tea and trying to get a moment's break from my toddler's relentless public love for me, and I see from the news on my phone that Jodie Foster has got married to a photographer called Alexandra, who used to date Ellen DeGeneres. As time passes, I see celeb mag photos of them with their arms around each other at parties. They look ecstatic. They are free. Marriage is legal and they have become the people who, as Jodie described to me when trying to discuss her last relationship, 'can have divorces'. They do not look like they're getting one any time soon.

10

And a fart at a party threatens to destabilise Los Angeles

Mal said I should go to this woman's birthday dinner with him, so I went. We both loved a party, and I vaguely knew the host. She worked in design and all her friends seemed to work in fashion and art and looked like models. Especially the ones who were models. They were nice and it was a balmy evening, the sort you always get in Los Angeles in, you know, *March*, and so we all sat down outside an Italian restaurant in Silver Lake and exhaled our days into the night air until the mood was giddy and the conversation was spilling everywhere. Wine was drunk and cigarettes were smoked (by them) and envy was felt (by me). Well, until the food came and I tucked into an enormous calzone, a great big beast of a folded pizza that the rest of them would never have dreamed of ordering.

I had never felt particularly self-conscious when eating decent amounts of food in LA – it made me feel like the millionaire at the table, dangling wheat- and dairy-based diamonds into my mouth – but now I had the best excuse in town. I was three months pregnant, which is the point when the doctors reckon you're past the riskiest stage and safe to start telling people beyond your closest family, even though you're not actually showing yet and could possibly go another month before anyone realises. And it was just as well that I wasn't showing yet, because my initial attempts to source maternity clothes had been an abject failure.

I'd been to the Grove, a very popular shopping centre, and walked into a couple of the big chain stores there to find their maternity section. Surprised that they didn't seem to have one, I'd been to the front desk to ask if they didn't make versions of their clothes for pregnant women, and heard, twice, that, oh yes, ma'am, they certainly did! Just not in the West Coast branches! I mean, *what*? Pregnant bodies only changed shape in Philadelphia? Perhaps moving back to London, something that people in London kept suggesting to me, wouldn't be such a bad idea after all.

I'd also been to a second appointment at the gynaecologist in Beverly Hills, who seemed to have fully recovered from the news that I owned a clitoris, and she had proceeded to warn me that eating for two was a myth that I was very much advised not to fall for. 'But I'm *starving*,' I had said to her, annoyed. 'You know how much extra food per day your body actually needs in pregnancy?' she had replied, and I thought, no, but I'm sure you're going to tell me. 'One glass of milk and half a banana,' she declared, factfully. I wanted to hate her but then she saw my face and her voice lightened. 'Look,' she added, 'I have a toddler myself, and I gained forty pounds during pregnancy, and let me tell you, not recognising your own body when you have a baby is no fun. The first year is hard enough without that estrangement.'

Something in what she was saying rang true, and a year later, a thousand miles away from her, I silently thanked her. Calzone aside, I somehow reined it all in.

So anyway, at this dinner I was telling people about the baby, even though it was a tricky story to announce because they'd say things like, 'Wow, Sophie I didn't even know you had a *boyfriend*!' and I'd keep smiling through my teeth while thinking *I don't*. Or I'd dance enigmatically around the truth because it was more fun than bursting into tears. Or I'd explain the truth, then ever so slightly burst into tears, just burst a little bit into tears, and then brush the tears aside as hormonal, when I knew they were factual.

I began to feel what it is to sit outside the narrative, trying to fit yourself into a fairy tale with some of the pages missing, one or two of the lead characters having gone astray. Sometimes I felt a surge of strength, that I was going to reinvent the fairy tale, goddammit. At other times I floated around the inside of the story as lost as a baby in the caul, wondering when the waters would break. Still, none of the beautiful people at the table were having a baby or had ever had a baby, so it definitely imbued me with a special power beyond fashion to have committed an act so un-narcissistic, and yet arguably the most narcissistic of all: the reproduction of myself. They were amazed!

When I first moved to LA I had thought that people like this were all effortlessly beautiful, because they looked so casual, with their hair just falling around like that, their skin so bare and dewy, their limbs naturally gangly and their clothes in unshowy neutral shades. My eyes had not yet adjusted to recognise the Natural Industrial Complex. This was the Goop heartland but just before Goop was invented, so it took me some time to realise that their bare skin was maintained with a four-step process of hundred-dollar creams every morning and night. That they paid extra for clothes in colours that my eyes could barely register, not bright, not white, just a grey-brown neutral that seemed to reappear in endless new formats. Fifty shades of greige. And that they would happily save the world by drinking the purest water flown in from Fiji and insist on drinking organic Californian wine at their wedding, only the wedding would turn out to be in Japan and the wine would all have to be sent there, the toxins emitted by the journey not being quite so important as they would end up in other, less healthy people's bodies.

I hadn't yet realised that one in particular of these women, with her pale, wan, dangly-armed schoolgirl chic, would drive to the gym every morning at 8 a.m. and instruct her personal trainer only to exercise her limbs in ways that maintained the gangly aesthetic, 'like *Gwyneth*'. That she once shouted at him, furious, when she thought some of her muscle work was starting to show: the whole point was that it shouldn't look like she had done any.

After the food had all been cleared and the gossip had been digested (had Drew Barrymore *really* broken up with a TV executive we knew after a celebrity magazine ran an article about him pushing the limits of the word *executive* and 'not even having his own parking space'), I needed to pee. I got to the loos and a few women from my table were already waiting in line to use the two cubicles. We were all quite excitable by this point, so they started talking about my baby again, wasn't it exciting, and ooh, could they rub my bump? This was the very first time it had happened, the patting of the belly, because – well – had I not been paying attention the last couple of days – I was starting to show now! Well how about that.

I had read other women's accounts of how they came to hate people coming up and touching them, but how could this be bad? It was wonderful, this roundening, this swelling of new. I felt great pride in having it. (This unlikely hypothesis of a baby, this late-night argument of new life, was entering the third dimension. It was becoming real. Oh my God. Look at it!) I flaunted my curves, as the *Daily Mail* would say, in those ladies' loos, and on that night the others all wanted to touch my flaunting. So three of them, with my happy permission, had a good pat of my burgeoning belly and they then insisted, when the next cubicle became available, that I must go ahead of them. And so I went in and I pulled my pants down and Christ alive. It must have been audible in the underground caves the Taliban were using in the Peshawar mountain range. It went on for longer than some Hollywood marriages.

That fart.

Finally, it stopped, but not before taking my bump with it. The bump was gone. I had been pregnant with pizza. People always say that you can't be 'a little bit pregnant', that it is purely binary, but that's exactly what I was. I was a *little* bit pregnant and a *whole lot* flatulent. I was actually more flatulent than pregnant, by a ratio of about 90 to 10 per cent. That swelling was not my child, it was my dinner, and now I had to get back outside.

All I remember, of making my way out of the toilets – the part of that memory that has not been swallowed whole by the shame – is that I stuck my tummy out like you do when you're pretending to be pregnant, only this was something of a new low, what with me actually being pregnant. I spent the rest of the evening smiling while trying to look as fat as humanly possible, which is something I've still not read about on Goop as a coping mechanism.

But sometimes when I'm feeling insecure, unsure of my role on this earth, or of my value, that fateful night comes back to me, and I think only this: I will never, ever be truly unhappy again. I will laugh, quietly and internally, for the rest of my life. I made some of the most beautiful people in LA rub my fart.

11

See, this is the thing about famous people

The thing about my family was that we all pretended to be a bit above celebrity, but none of us were at all. About once a year we would all go on a family trip to London where I prided myself on spotting a famous person every time. A presenter from a BBC travel show, a bad singer, Patrick Moore ordering a curry, Anthea Turner signing an autograph, someone from *Whose Line Is It Anyway*. The very idea that you could live in London and famous people would be walking around every single day, doing their shopping, ordering their curry, blew my tiny mind. I imagined living there and standing outdoors at all times in case I caught one. I came from a village, so the idea of the big city, and looking for celebrities in huge crowds, drugged me at a young age. Life became like my own personal ongoing game of *Where's Wally*.

Or I perceived celebrities like the kid from the Ready Brek advert with a glow all around them. Fame was that glow to me, that coating of specialness that meant nothing bad could ever happen to you, and that your mind would be free from doubt. I would read every interview with famous people that I could – they were my absolute favourite part of *Smash Hits*, along with the song lyrics so I could sing along and be more like them, know the exact words that they knew. I didn't want to read about the live concerts or how they made the film – I wanted to read what pop stars said about the minutiae of their lives, what thoughts went through their heads late at night and whether they shopped in supermarkets. I didn't want to know which designer made their clothes, I wanted to know what life event had given them pause. Because all their pauses and thoughts were, unlike mine, shielded by the golden rays, behind the golden line. They were wrapped up in something that made them safe, with the arms of others reaching out to catch them if they fell.

Years later, the lanky footballer Peter Crouch, when asked what he would have been if not a footballer, memorably replied, 'A virgin.' I interviewed his wife Abby Clancy some time after and mentioned that line. 'He still is,' she replied crisply, 'our daughter's adopted.'

12

Actually, I always thought I was a man

I knew I was having a boy. I knew from the moment the stick said P R E G N A N T that I was having a boy, and that he was strong like a wolf, so I decided to call him Wolf. There was this force field of masculine energy inside me, and before you write in to complain / start sniggering at the back there, no I can't explain what that was exactly – I just felt a power I had never felt before, and in the conversation between my gut instincts (wordless) and my rationalising brain (wordy) it became clear that I was carrying a manchild. Which put me in the brave new situation of being male and female at the same time, knowing that somewhere up the far northern reaches of my female sex organs I was growing a penis. And I liked it.

I liked having a penis and a vagina, with one of them having been caused by the misdemeanours of the other. I liked the mad maths of pregnancy. I liked how one dark night had led to the expansion of my physical form into something called a mother, or was it a spaceship, still too early to tell, and sometimes I even liked how a member of a new generation would be depending on me for responsible leadership and guidance, even though I had forged them out of whisky and lust. These were the kind of senseless equations I could bed myself down in. *Just like that*, as Tommy Cooper used to say – there it was, a brand-new life.

I liked sticking my belly out, having spent years walking past my reflection in shop windows and quickly sucking it in. I liked looking up at houses in the hills and imagining Wolf and I and maybe somebody else living up there one day, our floor covered in crayons, our dreams bouncing around the walls. Realistically, our beds would also need clean sheets and you probably couldn't, in all likelihood, wean a baby with burritos, but I'd get better at all that. I could do this. I could change.

I started thinking seriously about being both a mother and a father because the disagreement with Wolf's father was ongoing. I'm not going to describe it in detail, because these are people's real lives and this isn't only my story to tell. But safe to say it felt like being pulled in two directions at once: a new life taking me forwards into the future, some kind of ghost trying to pull me back to the past.

Being a mother and father, though, made a strange sort of sense to me. It was strangely similar to a feeling I had had for a long time, privately, and, ever since I could remember, I had been waiting to be found out. In my twenties, sitting in a university counsellor's office, I had once said out loud the thought that had preoccupied me for as long as I could remember, which was that behind my thick, dark eyebrows, there was a man. Or that I was a man. But not entirely me – it was the me who lived behind my thick, dark eyebrows. It was him. I can't make it any clearer.

And the counsellor was very nice about it, but what could she really say? I wasn't announcing myself as transgender, not that people were so aware of that at the time. There were no symptoms of schizophrenia. It was a duality I had been waiting to come out with all my life, and so I tried to explain that I had been running from the idea of womanhood since the age of about nine when I started to feel it coming for me and found I was unable to square myself with the idea, since I had these thick dark eyebrows, behind which I felt quite sure lurked a man.

But it wasn't a statement of fact, more a sentence of words. I didn't want to stop being the Sophie Heawood who was me. I liked her. I just wanted to understand the eyebrow person. I hadn't been through puberty when this began, and although I eventually wore a bra and started having periods, and sometimes boys fancied me, the female thing had still always felt like a sham on some level. I studied the art of being female like an anthropologist. I scrutinised girls and their behaviour. Their groups. And I mastered it, near enough, and I entered their groups, and I entertained their groups, because I was funny. And I just waited, really waited, for the day when somebody would look at me and go, wait a minute, I see you, I see you behind those eyebrows – you're not female after all.

In the 1990s, I left home and came to London, at a time of Britpop and drum'n'bass and the culture starting to tell us that you could still be a cute girl and drink like a drunk man, and so I did it with great gusto. I'd not actually been that much of a teenage boozer, and nor had I been all that bothered about it at university. But this newly ironicised lager culture, what with Britain having started to fetishise football, was a great place to stash an ever-growing suspicion that I wasn't like other girls at all. I hid my fear behind the bar in plain sight.

Around this time, I had one serious boyfriend, Ian, who came from Newcastle and carried himself as a trendy Geordie lad while quietly studying Japanese and playing the violin in a string quartet. He was very droll. I adored him. After a year and a half together, Ian admitted to me that he preferred men. We're still friends – he has lived as the gay man that he truly is ever since. But I can't say it did a lot for my confidence, or pride, to know that the sort of men who were attracted to me were not attracted to women. Ian wasn't the only gay man who grew very fond of me, or who came out to me when what I was hoping for was a declaration of love. The numbers seemed disproportionate. I must be a man. I drank more. I must be a man.

I drank a lot more. I would get my tits out at parties, be wild, suck another girl's tits in front of some guys, look at us, aren't we hot, aren't we female, aren't we something we're supposed to be. I don't know. Did the other girls even like it? Did I even fully have their consent? I became a bad influence on myself and on others in whose image I tried to recreate myself. Something that was made easier by the biggest invention of the decade, which wasn't spin doctors or the Spice Girls. It was the Wonderbra and it was deadly. Because, while designed to double up on your overtly feminine characteristics for the express benefit of men, it somehow served to make you even more macho. Which was the last thing I was looking for.

We became convinced by the marketing that Wonderbras made you bold, that they made you brassy. In fact, they bound you up like a Chinese footbinder and turned you into one of the titty, laughing lads. Oh, the subtle, cultural violence of the thing. The advert said 'Hello Boys' and that poster followed me everywhere; every magazine I read, every billboard I walked past in East London. Your tits weren't yours, they were for the men looking at you. Your body went from being a Thursday afternoon to a Saturday night, all the time sticking out like the Terminator's robot arm, like the shiny glass towers that were starting to rise up across London, and the mobile phone masts, like the long sharp shark that Damien Hirst had suspended in formaldehyde and that I stared at in the gallery, completely mesmerised. Sometimes I wonder if I was just drinking to take away the pain of the underwiring not fitting properly and digging into my chest cavity.

All the men I knew, meanwhile, were wearing T-shirts and Carhartt cargo trousers that were a bit too loose until they got a belt and then they were fine.

But now the years had passed and I had finally binned the Wonderbra and moved to California, where the constant sunlight had quietened down the man behind my eyebrows, and put me in a sundress with a kale salad and almost, almost, let me pass. Except that now I was having a baby, and accepting that you are a mother means first accepting you are a woman, and it is hard to say which I found more quietly monstrous. Still, I was excited about this big scan.

So Lily came with me to the gynaecologist's office, or as I now liked to think of that place, The Front Part. And at The Front Part I bared my belly for the gel and the scanning wand, and on the screen in front of us appeared some shapes that I wanted to be able to understand but honestly, all I could see were moving shadows on that display. It just looked like the grainy CCTV footage from inside Plato's cave. I couldn't tell what I was looking at.

But the doctor could.

'Do you see the heart, there?' she said, and then suddenly I could. A heartbeat arrived like a letter on the mat. Thud. And then another thud. Also my own.

'And over here …' she said.

I still couldn't see what we were looking for.

'Congratulations!' said the doctor. 'You're having a girl.'

And my heart stopped beating for a moment, and then recalibrated, like a sat-nav that understood that you had driven down a different street after all. And I went home and called my daughter's father, and he didn't answer and he didn't answer, and when he finally answered, it was bad. Not because she was a girl; he had always said she would be a girl, always, despite my insistence to the contrary. (Sometimes, in a curious way, it felt as if he knew her better than I did, and could see the future with more clarity. It was the weight of that knowing that seemed to overcome him, while I was buoyed by my own ignorance. There are things you have to not know, if you want to become a parent. You must dive into it like a fool.) It was bad, not because she was a girl, but because this was now real, and he was at sea, and didn't seem to want to get on the boat back to land, because the boat had sunk.

I knew then it was just me and her against the world.

13

And now I'm trying to hide from the police

I got an email from Fred, Sahil and Tom, friends who worked in the music industry in London, outlining their plans for staying with me in LA so we could all go to Coachella together. They said they'd be happy to share their hotel room and hire car with me for free if they could spend a few nights sleeping on my floor in LA before we set off for the desert near Palm Springs, and stressed that, because they understood I would be in the second trimester of my pregnancy, they just wanted to check which recreational drugs it would be all right for me to take. It was a joke. Just.

So the guys came and slept in my living room for a couple of nights. They brought with them London noise, gossip, stories of the new bands starting out and getting famous, the music industry whispers. Fred's own band had just been signed, and he was trying to impress American girls with his newfound confidence. 'To my great chagrin,' he would say to my friends, throwing the

French word into every conversation while looking like a suave Harry Potter, and I'd watch their faces crumble helplessly with love. I asked the boys what the main gossip was in our London music scene. 'Your pregnancy,' they replied.

They hired a car and Sahil drove us all the way to the desert, stopping only to get out and take group selfies beside particularly photogenic stretches of sand. The boys wore Ray-Bans and I wore an enormous straw hat, a denim dress and a bump. We got to the hotel in Palm Springs and decided what to do about the double bed and the sofa. Sahil said he would sleep on the sofa and somehow Fred, Tom and I said we would take the double bed. For some reason, probably to avoid fracturing the awkward masculinity of these two twenty-three-year-olds, I agreed to go in the middle.

Which meant that a woman with two swollen breasts and a third bump protruding from the centre of her body, who had to get up to pee several times in the night and who would no doubt be tossing and turning in the heat of the desert, air conditioning notwithstanding, would now be doing all of that in between two young men, one of whom she had only just met. I mean, it was fine. It was just that I was as horny as hell and had no chance of doing anything about it.

My God, the yearning. You have so much on the inside, pushing outwards, that in the interests of symmetry and basic laws of physics you feel a primal urge to be counterbalanced by something from the outside, pushing in. But no such luck. We all got to sleep eventually, the fan whirring overhead proving a neat counterpoint to the sound of my brain whirring inside my skull. ('Do you remember,' asked Fred, some years later, 'the sexual tension in that hotel bed?' How we laughed. I mean, I was relieved that somebody had finally said it.)

Anyway, American music festivals are strange. At British festivals, such as Glastonbury, you pitch a tent with your friends and camp out for several days, growing sunburned, starting to see warm lager as a vitamin, falafel wraps as your five a day. You can only face the festival loos every other day because it's like peering into the illustrations for Dante's *Inferno*.

You have moments of great joy when you peak on the drugs and realise that life is a great big adventure playground and you are whooshing down its slide. You then have moments of great agony when you come down from the drugs and realise that life is indeed a great big adventure playground, in which you are a thirty-seven-year-old who has lost all their friends and shat themselves in the miniature castle in front of someone called Michaela, who said she was a druid but really works in information resources in Kettering and is talking about the benefits of releasing pent-up emotional issues by drinking your own urine.

Then the next night you get back on the tepid lager and sing along to the choruses with all your friends and it's the best thing ever in your whole life, you and 60,000 other people raising your voices in song at the absolute guaranteed knowledge of what word and what notes are coming next. Somehow, that's where the magic releases itself deep into our collective psyche at the Great British singalong, the one day when we are all allowed to bellow our hearts out together, all of us tilting our heads back just a little because we are right under the skies and this is our most direct route to the gods. This is the religious part of the British festival experience – oh, and also getting so very lost at night that when you do eventually find your tent in a sea of other tents, the sight of it is distinctly similar to a miracle on the shores of Lake Galilee.

Then there are American festivals, such as Coachella, where you get a hotel room in one of the surrounding towns in the Palm Desert and Palm Springs area – everyone is scattered around a forty-mile radius – and you get in your big flashy jeep with your friends and you drive to the festival each day and then drive away again at night. The big quest at the end of each day is to locate which car park your vehicle is in and then sit patiently in a two-hour traffic jam to reach the exit and head onto the freeway. You're not allowed to bring booze with you into the festival itself, and there's only a couple of bars where you're allowed to buy it, after queuing up to prove your age to an officer, and you can't take the drinks with you to see an actual band. Understandably, everyone just turns up high on weed. The tickets cost a fortune and the Artist Passes are like gold dust, because artists, meaning the pop stars themselves, have places where they can drink, and they also get driven around the back of the stages in golf buggies so they can go and watch the show from the side and not enter the sprawling mosh pit with the commoners. So I had told the *NME*, who wanted me to review the festival for their British readers, hungry for gossip from the West Coast, that I could only do it if they got me one of these Artist Passes.

Now, I did not want to drink as I was religiously following the advice of my Beverly Hills gynaecologist who had said no way. But I did want to save my baby from getting moshed into an early labour, so I insisted I could only review the shows from the side of the stage. 'No problem!' said my editors, who had definitely never had to deal with a pregnant reviewer before. 'We can absolutely get you one of those!' and they absolutely did not.

So I got to the press check-in desk, found out the condition that I had set for taking the job hadn't been met, and decided, unbeknownst to my editors and the NME, that I would just have to review the gigs from somewhere quite far away from them, like, say a friend's dressing room, or the swimming pool at the villa Lily's friend had hired a couple of miles down the road, or from my hotel bed. I'm not proud of this. I had never, ever fabricated a review in my life before – my manic tendencies came to the fore when I was working and I'd be the person down the front with a notebook, frantically writing down every last thing that happened, not missing a trick. But by this point I was, to use the scientific term, a bit past giving a toss.

So I spent the festival protecting my bump and drinking coconut water in VIP, accidentally upsetting Paris Hilton (I told her that the meat on her kebab looked quite greasy and she then dropped it and ordered a different one) and sitting under my big hat looking winsome while people we all recognised walked past. And then there were the nights.

One night, after we'd all been to a pool party at the Ace Hotel after leaving the festival, it transpired that our designated driver Sahil had wanted one night off from being responsible, which seemed fair enough, given that he was young and single and had come all the way to the American desert to go to a party. So he got hammered. And the others, Fred and whoever had said that maybe they would drive, and I can't remember what happened, but then they all got drunk too and then we were left with no designated driver. Which would also have been fine if we hadn't been miles from our hotel, in the early hours of the morning, before the invention of Uber.

At which point everybody realised that I was, of course, completely sober, and so I would be able to drive us all home, hurrah. Now this is the part of the story where my memories diverge from those of the others who were present. I do not remember, at any time, claiming to have a driver's licence, or even any particular experience in driving a car. I feel confident that I almost definitely mentioned the fact that I had only ever had two driving lessons, both quite recently, in LA during my first trimester when I didn't dare tell my instructor that I was pregnant because it was before twelve weeks and I had taken that rule about not telling anyone rather literally. (Of course, you can tell a driving instructor, in fact, you can tell whoever you want, but at that point I believed all these instructions from my gynaecologist as if they were actual laws.)

I hadn't told the instructor that I was really feeling very sick indeed when he had whizzed me around Hancock Park during my first lesson, a lovely flat, posh area of Los Angeles designed around a lovely neat grid system where everything was slow and easy. Somehow, despite that day being the first time I had ever sat in the driving seat of a car – no Tesco's car park with my dad aged fifteen, no practising in a field, nothing – I had managed to do so well that for my second lesson, when the secret morning sickness was really kicking in, he had taken me straight onto the freeway. The 101 motorway that runs through Los Angeles. From there, he had me change onto four other famous freeways, maxing out the speed limit, all the time my eyes swimming in front of me as experienced American drivers sped past me, merging merging merging for two hours. I felt as though I would vomit onto the windscreen at any moment. I cancelled my lessons after that. It was too much.

There I was in Palm Springs a couple of months later, the sickness now having abated, as I was well into the second trimester when you actually feel lovely and sexy and quite fun, so I did think, yes, I can do this. But I'm pretty sure I told them I didn't entirely know how. They say I did, but they were gone. Anyway, we set out in this car, Sahil having to tell me how to turn the engine on, and me heading on down the main street on what felt like the wrong side of the road, because England was still imprinted on my brain.

It was a very long very straight road, lined by low, flat, modernist bungalows and glamorous shops. This was Palm Springs, a luxury retirement town for staid Californians

with money and a taste for comfortable mid-century archi-
tecture that had seemed quite futuristic in the 1950s. All
long straight lines and cruising speeds. This wasn't an
English town, with winding roads and hills and medieval
roundabouts to navigate – this was, almost literally, Easy
Street. Or so I thought until it dawned on me that I didn't
know what the buttons did, or that I was swerving as I
gained familiarity with the steering wheel, that my speeds
were either too low (would arouse suspicion) or too high
(would also arouse suspicion) and that I had to do something about that, which I was quite frantically trying to
do while trying to stay calm and putting up with the
jeering that was now coming from the customers of my
taxi, who were pissed and wailing that I had said I could
drive when clearly I could not. For my part I was calmly
telling them to shut the fuck up and that this would be
fine – that was, until we heard the siren and saw the flashing
light. Now, I still remained calm, because I didn't actually
know for sure that the police car pursuing us down a
darkened road specifically had anything to do with me.

Obviously, I've seen enough American telly to know
that what you're meant to do is pull over to the side of
the road, park the car, and get out with your hands on
your head before a corrupt and licentious officer gets you
frisked, breathalysed, and sent to jail. And I've seen
enough evidence that if you're black, you might not make
it as far as the jail, because the police are apparently
allowed to shoot you without ever facing any consequences. But I was white and British, and I'd never had
to learn those fears.

I was also, I can see now, already going into full-on Yorkshire Mum Mode, modelled on the behaviour of the women I grew up around in the north of England. In Yorkshire Mum Mode, there might be a drama erupting all around you but you just hoik up your bosom and think to yourself, oh *really*, we'll just see about this. In Yorkshire Mum Mode, you become a do-er. A solver. Someone who can handle anything, while disregarding small bureaucratic protocols that will only waste time, such as the law.

Thus I did what any self-respecting mother would do at this point in the unfolding drama. Having spotted what Americans would call a gas station ahead, closed for the night but with the forecourt wide open, I drove right into it, parked the car around the corner, and hid. We all sat there, waiting, until the police car had driven right past. And drive right past they did! It wasn't me they were chasing after all! The strange thing is that I don't remember this as stressful. Curious, yes, and definitely memorable, as anyone's first car drive without an instructor is bound to be. But emboldened by my new experience of being two people at once, it seemed I was growing more powerful by the day.

(Of course, Sahil did later get banged up in jail on a return trip to another American music festival, this time South by Southwest in Austin, Texas, when he was caught urinating in the street by the police and had to spend a night in the cells, leading to a #FREESAHIL Twitter campaign. But that is another story.)

14

And then my parents land in La-La Land

My parents came to stay at my apartment after a long and eventful flight which had culminated in my father falling out with the air steward for crimes against grammar. They arrived and looked at me as if I was a new species. My mother particularly seemed to be searching my form for clues. After a few days, she broke down – something about my laundry not being done. 'I thought you'd be *different*,' she burst out. Sadly for her, despite feeling more powerful about breaking the law in cars, and rattling through some to-do lists, I was exactly the same person at home that I had been before having drunken unprotected sex while feeling emotionally vulnerable and ovulating. My mother had imagined that pregnancy would transform me, but so far the chaos continued much as it had before, and I wasn't even drunk. It was almost as if this was my personality.

We went to look at a few new apartments to rent as I had decided I would have to leave my one-bedroom flat and get one with a second bedroom, ideally not up two flights of stairs, especially as my mother had offered to come out to stay for the first few months of the baby's life and help, which would be an absolute godsend. I wasn't entirely sure how I was going to pay for a bigger place, especially when I couldn't really do my job, and none of the landlords were exactly thrilled about the idea of a pregnant single freelancer on a restrictive overseas visa signing a contract with them. Also, the fact I would go on viewings and start trying to haggle down the price, telling them I was 'a bit worried about work at the moment' possibly didn't help my cause too much, now I come to think about it.

It is no wonder then that my parents, after a week of examining this situation, suggested that I really, truly might want to think about coming home. The more they said this, the more sense it made, even though I couldn't bear it. I lived in California now. *This* was my home, wasn't it? But the more viewings I went on, the more I started to feel like Mary trudging through Bethlehem trying to find room at the inn. My own landlord was extremely nice to me, knowing, as she did, that I was a good tenant who paid my rent on time (just), and a nice person. 'You can always just stay here,' she used to say, 'the baby will probably sleep in your room for the first year anyway, and look, you've got plenty of space.' It's true, my living room was a decent size. I was happy there. But something in me seemed to say, you have to change, things must change. I had to make some kind of external physical progress to match the internal one. I had to lose. I had to shed my old life like an unwilling snake.

15

And my friends throw a baby shower

Lily wanted to throw me a baby shower. First I was afraid, then I was mortified. Wasn't sure I could handle this American outpouring of infant-related sentimentality. I was carrying a small wolf, not a knitted product. This was not a situation that Hallmark Cards could fix. On the day itself, I turned up at the house where Lily had arranged to hold the party, and my worst fears were confirmed. I mean, don't get me wrong – I was overwhelmed by the lengths they had gone to. So many people I loved were there waiting for me, and they had decorated the whole house pink with streamers and ribbons and balloons. Pink. Wow. It dawned on me at this point that even the most liberal pockets of big American cities can still be very different from London, where I doubted that most of my friends would care much about the baby's gender, or hold much truck with the idea that, if you were having a girl, everything had to be the colour of a perky vulva.

Our friend Jenny, a professional baker, arrived with the most beautiful cake, which the others admitted they had been tempted to ask her to ice with the words 'And baby makes two'. Which made everyone laugh, because baby was supposed to make three, which made me want to burst into tears, which felt much more appropriate.

And there were games, including one where Lily had bought a box of twenty-five blank gift cards and numbered them, and everyone at the party would write a birthday message to my child for the next twenty-five years of her life. And so they did. They wrote messages about what I was like, about what they thought she might be like, about Los Angeles in 2011. One of them took a Polaroid photo of me in my stripy sundress, my big straw hat and my bump, and put it straight into the envelope with a note that said, look, here you are inside your mama!

I was given the cards to read out and then it dawned on me, somewhere around card number six or seven, that this was a community of people who all wanted to raise my baby with me. That being a single parent didn't mean you and the kid against the world, it meant bringing everyone in. It takes a village, they said in cheesy America, to raise a child, and oh my God I felt it now. We were the village, all of us, right there in the sunshine, in the love. They loved me, and they loved the person who was yet to come. They were on our team and they were game. And I was leaving, to go back to London and live alone in the rain.

The way the decking was organised in the garden created a natural sort of stage, so I stood on it and addressed all my friends who had gathered there. They were a mixture of those who believed the universe had a plan for all of us, as if the universe were some kind of interplanetary careers advisor, and those who believed the universe was a collection of rocks hurtling through space, upon which we would all ruin, and then die, and then rot, and none of the rocks would ever give a shit, because they were rocks.

But we were all friends together, because there is something in the quality of the light that falls over Los Angeles that can unite the universers with the chapter-and-versers in a glorious throng. And so I told them something I had noticed in my pregnancy, which was that my due date had been a matter of hugely different reaction from my friends in different parts of the world. You see, my due date was September the 11th, which was obviously quite a resonant date in recent American historical memory. And the first people I had told about my pregnancy were English, because they were my nearest and dearest and needed to know first. And after they had all got over the shock of all the rest of it, and the last thing left to discuss was the due date, they would giggle a bit when I told them it was September the 11th, or 9/11 as the Americans called it. It seemed to release the tension in every conversation – there I was, having a catastrophically unplanned baby all the way over in America and I'd chosen the tenth anniversary of the most calamitous and deadliest terror attack in the US to do it on. Brits like to laugh at inappropriate things. How we laughed.

Obviously, when I told American friends from New York, they didn't laugh at all. Why would they? The attacks were still a very recent memory, and some of them had seen it happen first hand. They all said the same thing, nervously, 'You know what … babies never come on the due date. First babies are always late. Or early. It just *won't* be that date.'

But when I told the people who surrounded me in Los Angeles, a third and completely new reaction occurred. As I told the Californians my big news, that some strange miracle had gifted me this baby, and that it was due to proceed from my loins on 9/11, their eyes would light up.

'A VIRGO!' they would cry out joyfully.

Anyway, I was just re-telling this anecdote to my friends on the stage at my baby shower and everyone was laughing, even the people who had said 'A VIRGO!' the first time around, and even the ones who read the *New York Times* every day and made sure to vote in every election and couldn't actually believe the others could be so moronic, when another friend turned up late to the party and walked in to hear the bit where I said the baby was due on September the 11th. 'Oh!' she burst out. 'A Virgo!'

I have never felt so vindicated in my life. Not even when I eventually went so far overdue that I gave birth to a Libran.

PART TWO

London

I wake up on a sofa surrounded by dead animals in Dalston

Properly surrounded by them. Stuffed animals. I don't mean teddy bears. I mean that a taxidermied lioness, a stuffed pet hedgehog (alas, poor Gilbert), a collection of monkey skulls, a cassowary skeleton and the foetus of an actual human baby in a jar were all staring me in the face as I lay on the sofa, coming round to my new surroundings and wondering if that really was an elephant's foot being used as a recycling bin. For a couple of days, after first arriving back in London, I had been living in this warehouse flat belonging to my friend Wynd and sleeping in his spare bedroom. But another friend, Wade, was also in town and staying there too, as he often did, causing Wynd to hang up a sign on the front door saying 'Where there's a Wade there's a Wynd', which sat just below the sign saying 'Alcoholics Conspicuous, Hackney Branch, weekly meetings every

Mon, Tues, Wed, Thur, Fri, Sat & Sun, bring vodka.' The night before, Wade had arrived home with a Swedish nineteen-year-old wearing jeans tight enough to sterilise a dog, so for some reason, perhaps because I was preparing to look after a child myself, and thus felt understanding of his burden, I told Wade that he and his young friend could have my bed.

It was more of a mattress on the floor anyhow, up a folding ladder through a trap door in the kitchen ceiling into the attic, where you had to stoop or hit the roof, so it was better suited to their horizontal endeavours. I slept on the kitchen sofa, which was surrounded by shelves of dead animals belonging to Wynd. I've known him ever since we hung out at the same nightclub years ago, the place where I met most of my close friends, none of whom have anything one might describe as a normal job. Wynd took his genuine passion for strange objects and outsider artists and became an art dealer of sorts, favouring grotesque embalmed creatures and barbarous taxidermy, which he puts in a shop he rents on the dirtiest bit of Mare Street in Hackney, and where TV crews from around the world come to interview him about why he sells them. Sometimes, on occasion, he even sells them.

You might think that it was lonely sleeping in a kitchen, but if the post-truth and post-death animals weren't company enough, there was the soundtrack of Wade and the Swede shagging in my bed through the trapdoor above us, and if I still felt unaccompanied, there was the siren song of the emergency services wailing their vehicles down the high street from Homerton Hospital, because of an inner-city stabbing or a suspected suicide bomb.

In California, they talk a lot about living in the present moment and focusing on the now, rather than worrying about what is past or yet to come. They're right of course, and yet ironically, it is a spiritual practice that I find much easier to accomplish in London, where there is so much more *now* to worry about, all day and all night, that you barely have any time to stress out about the rest of it.

The building, like so many in the area, was an old factory, where Victorian girls and their mothers would make slippers or oil cloths or matches to light fires and cigarettes, working for fourteen hours a day, perhaps dipping slivers of wood into white phosphorus to make the match, its poison working its way into their faces, making their skin glow in the dark, turning their vomit fluorescent and necrotising their jaws away. Wynd would probably have collected some of their rotten jaws if anyone had cared enough to keep them, and I would probably have gone through fourteen agonised stages of ethical argument about them with him, before he'd admit he'd actually made them from papier mâché.

I often reasoned with myself about how much we were part of the problem; art wankers living in an area where most people couldn't afford to be art wankers. We were happy to live with gaps and cracks in buildings that had sat empty for years alongside estates more full of life, but when the artists moved in, the development money followed, and then there was trouble for the original local residents. All around us, local shops and small unflashy businesses grew ever more encroached upon by new developments, which tended to take old industrial buildings and turn them into luxury flats that nobody from this area could ever afford to buy. They weren't run by art wankers, but by whole committees of wankers, the sorts who could rebrand Holloway Prison as an 'exclusive gated community' and who always insisted on marketing the 'industrial' nature of the building's heritage, even though the most industrial thing any of the new property owners would probably ever do was lay off 427 employees of a factory they'd never visited during their day job as a management consultant. The heaviest lifting they undertook was moving their mortgage to a different bank.

There were a pair of these poncey new developments down the road from us, called Arthaus and Monohaus. Personally, I always hoped they would be followed by Acidhaus and Hardhaus, and after that Happyhaus and Handbaghaus, but sadly I am waiting still. I didn't want the luxury anyway. I liked big cracks in big windows, letting the whole city in, singing its dirty great hosannas at us all. I hadn't wanted to leave sunshiney California, but now that I had, my soul was forced to admit that it had come home. I was back in my rightful land of dirt.

And if all that still wasn't enough to remind me that all human life was here, or at least near, then there was the foetus that had been growing inside me for nearly six months now, even though I still hadn't felt it kick. I worried so much about its lack of kick that I felt quietly terrified that it, that she, was a duff, a dud, a dead baby.

I did so want a live one, now, to call my own – I had grown very attached to the idea. But I had to take my mind off it. I wanted to go out.

Somebody texted to say there was a party in Dalston, a gig that night, and that they didn't suppose I'd be interested but just thought they would ask? Oh, I was interested. I was more interested in going than I was in breathing. My days were spent doing bits of freelance journalism, going to midwives' appointments and traipsing around estate agents trying to find a place where I and this new person could live once it stopped living in me. The irony of my own body functioning as a cosy bedroom when I didn't have one was not lost on me.

The housing search wasn't going very well because I baulked slightly when they asked for references and wage slips and job contracts and credit ratings and all the other stuff that didn't come easily to a freelancer who'd been living overseas somewhat carelessly. Not to mention the moment where they would inevitably gaze at my burgeoning body and enquire when my husband would be bringing in his reference forms too, and would he be at the viewing? Having been turned down for all those LA rentals after explaining that I worked freelance and was having a baby on my own, I wasn't about to make that mistake again.

'He doesn't mind!' I would sometimes say. Or, doing my best Stepford Wife face, 'He trusts me to choose!' 'He's away a lot,' I'd sometimes mutter, and at times, I'd add in entirely needless, imaginary details about this fantastical man, who in reality wasn't coming to live in the house, but had been very encouraging of the idea of me moving to London. Aside from the fact that he didn't even like America, he was based in Europe and so we would be much nearer to each other. Now that he had accepted that this baby was very much reality, the Musician had come round to the idea of us forming some kind of modern, part-time family arrangement where we would be divided only by a Eurostar, rather than an entire ocean. Things could still get unpleasant between us at times, but the reality of the situation had at least been accepted by both of us, and he had urged me to leave LA so he would be better placed to join in with our child's life. And so I could have a baby for free on the NHS, rather than in a system where they wheeled the credit-card machine to your bed. Estate agents would ask me to fill in a form including the phrase 'Relationship status' and there was never enough space to describe something that resembled the football match that soldiers on the Western Front played against the Germans in no-man's-land on Christmas Day. We were a white flag, at this moment, flapping limply along.

The gig was on the Strip, which meant the part of Kingsland Road in Dalston, just up the road from Shoreditch, where all the scuzzy hipster bars were to be found, and where my younger friends, still in their twenties, liked to get drunk. It was a section of a long Roman road, part of the Old North Road, in fact, that Dick Turpin used to ride along on his trusty horse, committing highway robberies, even when there was a price of £100 on his head. The people who now rode the Strip in mini-cabs also had a price of £100 on their heads, but only due to the daylight robbery of their hairdressers. I couldn't go out with friends my own age – they were all busy having babies. They stayed in with their husbands and watched box sets, or deliberated over which of their unborn IVF twins to call Flotsam and which to call Jetsam, ending in seething rows about whether Jetsam was a girl's name. I might be exaggerating. But I felt more at home with people who could barely decide if they were boys or girls themselves, and so I wanted to go to the Strip, even though I couldn't drink, even though my friends only ironically referred to it as the Strip because, though equally full of bars, it was absolutely nothing like the Sunset Strip in LA. Even though this was a joke I found particularly painful.

All right, so they both had their good points. The Sunset Strip in LA had palm trees and pools and cocktails and light and aspiration, sure, but here in the dark, wet Dalston equivalent, you could drink ten pints and then shit yourself and your friends would still like you. I knew this because another friend of ours had done exactly that, and he explained to me afterwards how he had nearly been in the toilet cubicle when it happened, and so had managed to get it together enough to phone one of our other friends to come and rescue him and his trousers. His girlfriend was American and through her he had also spent a lot of time in bars in New York. 'And it's bollocks when they say Americans are friendlier than us, because the people I've met in New York would *never* look after you if you drank ten pints and shat yourself. They'd think you were a loser,' he mused.

As well as the night-time venues – the big Turkish snooker hall Efes, the scruffy bar Bardens, which had gone inexplicably shiny and posh, and the basement gig venue Skelter with its walls covered in old punk newspapers – the Strip also contained daytime coffee shops where people sat with their laptops, eking out the dregs of one hot drink for four hours so they could exploit the free Wi-Fi for which they had memorised today's password, ChocolateSaltyBalls69. People would sit around staring vaguely into their screens, ignoring the people who sat all around them to have conversations with people unseen, which made the whole vibe quite a lot like an old people's home. Except it was a young people's home, offering supported daycare for the jejune. Senile dementia is when you can't remember if the conversation you were just in the middle of was taking place on the Queen Mary, the Pope's bedroom or in the garden of a house you last visited in 1965; juvenile dementia is when you can't remember if the conversation you were just in the middle of was taking place on WhatsApp, Slack or the direct messaging bit of your third and most niche Instagram account on which you post only selfies taken in the light that comes from inside the door of your fridge.

And so the customers all stared at their MacBooks and their iPhones, finally achieving twenty minutes of productivity after an initial three hours of preparativity, which meant reading the internet in its entirety just in case anyone, anywhere had added anything to it. (One must, after all, remain vigilant at all times.) And all of these people were freelance, which meant they could work free of uniform and free of office hours, which meant they were never off work, because they were never at work. They were also free of trade unions and HR support, free of an annual salary, holiday leave, sick pay or maternity cover or a pension, and thus they were also free of a future. They were not so much freelance as self-unemployed. They were fun-employed. And they were me. Weightless. We were the floating world, and when a strong wind came we would blow away entirely. Only I had to do something about this baby that was coming. And I would. Soon.

People in the basement bar were bumping into each other. The band was laying down some urban ennui, designed to please some algorithm or other, only more loudly. The venue was hot and noisy and threatened to envelop me in a way which I yearned for. It was like being hugged by a place, just the sort of claustrophobia that I long for, that brings me back to myself by taking my choices away. I wonder if that's what it's like being a foetus, trapped in a hot noisy basement with no windows, swooshing around in liquids. This is what it's like in all the bars I've ever loved, and at the bottom of all of them, however pretentious or cool or uncool the crowd, are beating little hamster hearts inside every body, inside every presented self in the room, and every little hamster heart pounds along to the music with the words *love me, love me, love me.*

And I do love them. I love my friends. I love them and I miss them, even when I'm with them. Sometimes I go to the toilet at one of these nights out, and when I'm sitting on the toilet I scroll through my phone and I start seeing pictures on Instagram of people I know having another night out, and I feel a great rush of FOMO, the Fear of Missing Out, and I wish I was having that fun, even though it's the people I'm with who've posted photos of the night out we're all on, three feet outside this toilet door. I can never quite make myself feel that I'm having the same night out as the people I'm with. There's a need to get even more squashed. Bring their hamster hearts closer in.

Tonight, though, they were close, and when somebody suggested a limbo-dancing competition I felt so alive that I entered it. There was cheering and I won, though perhaps not by any rigorous measure, or with there actually being a real barrier – just somebody wobbling their arm above me as I nearly toppled over. And then the DJ played a song called 'The Rat' by the Walkmen and everyone sang along, singing their little hearts out, and I was happy for the first time in a long time. Surrounded by my holy congregation, our sacred rituals, reunions. This was where we worshipped and this was where I wanted to live. They say it takes a village to raise a child, and it does. It's just that my village was pissed.

Fred, who I had shared a bed with at Coachella and driven for, asked me how I was feeling. Special, was the answer. I felt special. I liked sticking out my belly, liked pushing it out instead of sucking it in like I'd been doing since I was thirteen. The awful inhaling I'd been doing, trying to look thin. It was big now. It was famous. It felt like being pregnant with a celebrity. My body was thick with fame. There were never any of these bumps in these bars. But that meant that people all wanted to ask me the same four questions, in the same order, every time, and it had been going on for a couple of months now and I didn't mind. They'd ask how far gone I was, and if I knew the sex, and then ask if I'd picked a name, and then they'd ask the due date. For some reason, it was always those four questions, in that same order, ending in my September the 11th punchline. I knew the drill. I liked the drill. I didn't even mind people rubbing the bump without permission, even though no millennial ever rubbed the bump without asking, because they were all super woke politically and knew that a woman's body was her private property, which was a shame, because I longed for them to touch me.

The four questions had been going so well until that night. Until I was introduced to someone called Wafa, whose name rang a bell I couldn't quite place. She looked pretty cool – maybe she was a minor pop star. Maybe I'd read about her. She gave out good vibes and was instantly friendly, wanting to know how pregnant I was. 'Do you know if it's a boy or a girl?' she asked next, and I answered, only then my stomach lurched. Then she asked me if I had picked a name, and I must have answered her, but I don't remember, because my brain was rapidly scrambling for a different answer to the fourth question that I knew was coming. Of course, I could have just made up a date, but in those few seconds all I could think was – I am going to say September 11th, out loud, or maybe I'm going to say it the American way, 9/11, and either way, it is coming, it is coming *fast*. Only then my friend Sahil came back and gave her a drink or something, interrupting us, and the conversation was suddenly lost in some kind of actual *miracle*, as if the gods themselves had intervened.

And Wafa never got to ask for my due date, and for that I was grateful for eternity, because I knew now where I recognised her from. It was an article in a men's mag about this hot young woman who had grown up in Switzerland and now wanted to be a singing modelling muso, but who was struggling with a mixed public perception of her budding career, just because she was Osama Bin Laden's niece.

Only in fucking Dalston.

And then it was nearly 1 a.m. and my friend Eva said she was tired and going home, she and her boyfriend couldn't understand how I was still going. Wasn't pregnancy exhausting? How do you do it, I'm more tired than you are, she said. And I beamed at her, and waved them off, and swallowed and said nothing. Because it turns out that you don't need any stimulants to stay out late, and you don't need to have any energy left in your body either. You just need to be more afraid of going home to a place where the only person who looks at you is in the mirror.

17

And I attempt to revive my career in the British media by hiding in a lavatory

I hadn't worked in London for two years, and I might have had a pretty good set-up with my Hollywood journalism but it had taken me those two years to establish that slot. Now I was back in London, I was terrified. Newspapers and magazines were having a recession all of their own, with freelance writers and photographers losing their regular work, which would be given to in-house staff, only for the in-house staff to then lose their jobs too. My beat was entertainment, and I was quick to make it clear that I wasn't a real journalist when introduced to new people who looked like they'd get cross about my silly job. 'I'm not a reporter, I do the fun stuff,' I'd say, pre-empting their disapproval. It was fine by me if they thought it was trivial – I'd grown up watching my social worker mother deal with child abuse in so many families, trying to differentiate between intentional neglect and the side effects of abject poverty; and removing children from their homes if she could prove at enough legal stages that they were in genuine danger. She also worked on political campaigns to stop that poverty occurring in the first place. I couldn't have done what she did. I knew I wasn't cut out for the hard stuff.

Instead, I had become the fun person that an editor could dispatch onto an international flight at the last minute, because I was always up for an adventure and didn't have a spouse who'd be annoyed about it. I'd go on tour with bands, do the interviews on their druggy tour buses in the early hours, and write it up like a student with an essay crisis as the sun was rising. I had studied languages at university so I could switch into French if an electronic musician in Paris was being particularly recalcitrant in English (i.e., literally every time I spoke to a French musician). I'd been around Brazil interviewing local musicians in Portuguese and had written about Latin American stars by talking to their fans in Spanish. I wasn't word perfect in any of these languages, but in the moment, in person, I could pull it out of the bag. And after that, I had felt confident enough to sort out my own American work visa and base myself in LA for all Hollywood needs, making my editors' lives easier. Which was just as well, as it wasn't as if I knew a whole lot about the film industry or as if I had even sat through more than about five car-chase scenes in my life – truth be told, I only really loved arty French films, as the intellectual stimulation in them was so much better, by which I mean the sex scenes. But Hollywood wowed me, because it was fame itself that I loved.

Nobody had the budgets to fly journalists out much at that time, so basing myself in the Hollywood heart of the action had been a stroke of genius. But what was I going to write about now I was going to be stuck on my own in Hackney with a baby? I didn't want to just sit and rattle off my opinions about famous people from a distance – there seemed an inevitable bitchiness to that kind of writing, and writing bitchily, though I was capable of it, made me feel low. I'd tried just being a reviewer of songs years before, which was something you could largely do from your living room, but using 400 words to eviscerate an album I didn't like when people had spent two years of their life creating it out of thin air didn't feel right to me either. So what was I going to do? I was about to have a baby, I had no fixed abode, and I was cohabiting with Dr Dolittle's cast of backstreet abortions.

So when someone on *The Times* arts desk asked if I'd like to cover the launch of a new pop music magazine aimed at tweenage children, I said yes immediately. Even though, once I had spent twenty seconds reading through the magazine's marketing proposal, I could see with utter clarity that this project was a poorly conceived, completely unrealistic proposal that would definitely fold after two issues, while also realising that I knew far more about this than my editor and needed to explain to her why magazines couldn't currently launch to this age bracket with this agenda and these people running it. I didn't say any of this, of course. I said I'd go and meet the makers of this new kids' magazine in West London the next day, how absolutely wonderful.

Of course I ended up running late. I was unpunctual at the best of times, and this was not the best of times. I had a big bump attached to my front that slowed the central navigation system, plus I hadn't had to navigate rush-hour traffic in central London in years. So after my tube train suddenly got cancelled and we were all kicked off it, I waddled up the three flights of stairs and hailed a black cab that I could in no way afford. The cab went through Hyde Park and past the Serpentine Lake, beautiful parts of London that should have been such a treat, with the sort of views that are be devoured by American tourists. And I almost felt like an American tourist at this point. But my gut was beginning to incubate a sense of panic, and then it turned out there were speed bumps and cattle grids in the road through the park.

This was one of those old, rackety black cabs in desperate need of re-upholstering, the sort whose driver has rangey eyes and a mouth that says, 'I'm not racist but.' So the suspension went BOOM BOOM WHOP every time we went over one of these things. I had never been car sick before, but pregnancy was testing that claim to its outer limits and then a bit beyond them. The more I thought about the interview ahead, the more I struggled to think of one single question to ask these magazine types. Looking back now, it seems obvious that anyone launching a new product has loads to tell you about it without much prodding, and all you have to really ask is why this, why now, why you, but my mind was turning to a blankness in which I was surely going to be sick, while the meter was racking up a fare I couldn't pay.

I remember it now, seven years later – the desperate feeling, that fear, of something slipping away from me in that taxi. Perhaps it was my career.

The receptionist at the big corporate office building where the tweenie popsters had rented a floor told me to go up to Level Five. By the time I got to Level Five I was able to get out of the lift, but I was not able to walk through the double doors into the office. The doors were a few feet away from me; they seemed as distant as Mars. They seemed to hate me more than Mars did. There was a toilet on the landing and somehow I got in there and into a cubicle, where I slumped on the lavatory, shaking. Out of everything that humankind has created while thinking, 'ach, this'll be all right', the corporate grey windowless toilet is surely the point where your soul says, 'you know what, maybe it won't?' The toilet confirmed my new belief, rapidly gathering traction with my body, that all life was futile. Abandon hope, all ye who piss here.

After a while there was a knock. Somebody else wanted the loo. They had been waiting but I don't know how long I'd been in. A few seconds? Twenty minutes? 'Are you all right in there?' she asked, to which I of course had to murmur 'Yes' when the real answer was, 'I just gave my mind to the toilet pan, the future is bullying me, the walls are joining in.' I exited and she entered. Then I sat myself down on the floor beside the sinks, and after she left the room altogether I just about managed to use my mobile phone to ring the people I was supposed to be meeting and say I would unfortunately not be able to do the interview because I had been taken ill. Oh, they said, but you're here aren't you? Because they rang us from the front desk about ten minutes ago to say you were on your way up?

Well. The thing is, I said. The thing is. I've been taken ill in the toilets. I'm in them now but I'm leaving. Soon. And then I don't know exactly what happened after that, if it was the toilet lady or the phone lady who came to pick me up and take me into the office against my will, to look after me. If they were the same person. Because what happened was that they didn't look after me. They placed me in a very bright meeting room, a perfect goldfish bowl, that overlooked a major shopping street. And then, while I struggled for breath and a place in my mind to call my own, they brought in everyone I had been scheduled to meet, a whole team of people who sat around me, looking at me, saying how sorry they were that I didn't feel able to do this interview. I mean, you *can* see it from their point of view – they've been told that a writer from *The Times* newspaper, which is still a really big deal, is coming to cover their start-up venture and put them in the paper of record, read by the leaders of our great nation. And what they get is a massively pregnant lady who has settled down to roll around on their lavatory floors while thinking she is an egg. It was like the Mad Hatter's Tea Party, only I was now seated at a long oval table, surrounded by expectant media wankers dressed in asymmetrical neons. I was the dormouse and I was the teapot. My American brain told me I was drowning; my British brain told me it would be rude to mention it. And they all wanted to talk, which was ironic, because if I'd been in any fit state to talk I'd have turned on my tape recorder and got paid for doing the interview. I wasn't going to get paid for cancelling, so there was no way I was talking to these smiling fuckers for free. I just wanted to die, really, which was handy, because a part of me was convinced I already had.

And then some kind person said, Is there anyone I can contact for you, and I thought oh God yes, Lily, please God, Lily, who was in London staying with her sister for a couple of months. I don't remember who rang her – was it me? – but she said she would stop what she was doing immediately and come to get me. About half an hour later she walked into that room with her gorgeous red hair and gorgeous big smile and it was the most beautiful sight I had ever seen in my life. It remains the most beautiful sight I have ever seen in my life, and I have a daughter now. Lily got me out of there, took me into the cafe next door and fed me roast potatoes and gave me wine, even though I hadn't touched alcohol in six months, even though she was teetotal herself, even though she was a nature goddess type who believed in raw green leaves and hiking and crystals and talking to dead people through the medium of squirrels. She got me a glass of something red, after pretending to the waiter that it was for her then slipping it across the table to me, not that he gave a toss either way, thank fuck for London, and I came back to life. The potatoes helped too.

'You've had a panic attack,' she said, cheerfully.

This was entirely new information to me. I wasn't mad. I wasn't losing it. I'd had my first ever panic attack and now I was recovering. That was just a thing that could happen. Oh!

18

The loneliness of the long, distant antenatal class

I moved from Wynd's kitchen sofa into the flat next door, because someone else in the building had gone away for a week and it was empty. This flat didn't contain any dead things, but it was overflowing with art. Big, colourful pieces of ambitious, unfinished art, all made by someone whose mind sometimes overtook him in a frenzy. He had a sleeping platform up in a sort of eyrie that he had constructed from junk, which overlooked the whole flat. You couldn't really even look over the room, in any one direction, without feeling your own mind overtaking you. It was like a deconstructed circus; a drunk and angry maze. I don't remember any windows. It was like a Bohemian reconstruction of my toilet panic attack.

The eyrie was kind of amazing though, and I slept in a bed there surrounded by books about the occult. For some reason, life had brought me an awful lot of men who liked Aleister Crowley, and I just want to issue a warning now to any woman considering getting involved with one. Yes, it's fascinating to read about magic, or magick as the 1920s occultist Crowley called it, and yes, it's great to step outside this world we live in and open your eyes to wild, counter-cultural ideas. The only thing is, back in this world in which you're still going to have to sleep, the man who gets deep into Crowley will probably also believe himself to be above such petty cultural norms as 'washing up', 'ringing you back' or 'fidelity'. He will unfailingly turn out to be an egocentric with a selective interest in 'the truth' and an even less convincing interest in 'listening to a word you say' or even 'fully believing that women also count as people'. He won't vote for any of the main political parties, which is fine, except that he'll be half Green and half Trump and you won't ever really know which. He might even, and this is your final warning, use the word 'libtard'. And one day you'll be sleeping in his bed in which he has never made you come, amid a pile of literature about the all-seeing third-eye and the Hermetic Order of the Golden Dawn, and you'll wonder what the fuck has happened to your life.

The Musician was in France at this point, and there were some days when we would email back and forth, friendly enough, joking around a bit. I said that I'd tried everything to make the baby kick, and that even though the scans showed everything was normal and she was definitely alive in there, the placenta had got positioned in a way that was stopping me from feeling anything, and I wanted to feel her so desperately. Why don't you, he said, play her some music I know she's going to react to – why don't you play her Glenn Gould's Goldberg Variations!

Gould was a Canadian pianist who had died in the 1980s, and the Musician told me that the guy had been an absolute maverick, about whom people still spoke in hushed, reverential tones. How he did classical music his own way, singing and muttering his way through his recitals of instrumental pieces. How purely he inhabited the music of Bach. How he used to practise piano pieces inside his mind, from memory, saying he didn't know why others spent so many hours actually touching the keys. He thought concerts were evil, wanted to ban applause and often cancelled shows at the last minute; a paranoid hypochondriac who hated to be touched. Now I think about it, he was probably into Aleister Crowley.

The Goldberg Variations were a series of short pieces written by Bach for the harpsichord, with all of its spindly plinky-plonkiness, (yes, those are the official terms), so they were difficult to play on the piano, but the mad bastard Glenn Gould had not only done it but nailed it. So then my mad bastard Musician sent me an mp3 file of the one he thought I should play to raise our child from her slumber, and I sat in yet another mad bastard's art eyrie and played it from my computer into big headphones that I held right against my bump. And do you know what? It bloody well mad bastard worked. BOOF. There she kicked! Possibly telling me to turn it the fuck off.

I began attending antenatal classes, where the husbands and boyfriends were taught all the helpful things they could do for us pregnant women during pregnancy, labour and the first few months of parenthood. I'm sure the class was billed as something more comprehensively about babies in general, but I experienced it solely as a guide to heteronormative marriage practices, with me the only single person there, feeling like the extra prick at a wedding. Except that the two things I most demonstrably lacked were a) a prick and b) a wedding.

And so every Wednesday for a couple of months in my late pregnancy, I would spend the day steeling myself for an evening spent hearing, 'And now I'll show you a lower back rub that partners can give to really help with the pain of contractions – *Sophie, I'll be your partner for this.*' A room full of nice men would then do nice things to make the women they'd nicely inseminated feel a little nicer about it all, and the nicer they made them feel, the worse I felt. I was the odd number in a room full of evens, sat there on my cushion like the square root of a couple, like the square root of a family. Like I had been divided by myself.

Of course, this shouldn't have been a thing in open-minded Hackney in the twenty-first century. I was hardly being forced into a home for unmarried mothers and having my baby adopted against my will. Technically, I had nothing to feel ashamed of – but you try telling that to a lower back that longs to be rubbed. There is a cultural residue that seeps through the generations long after the public narrative has moved on. It leaks like ink into our lives, all the more so when we live alone with nobody to wash it off us. Public narratives and private stories are two different countries, divided by a sea called shame.

And shame is tidal; at certain times it wells up and surges onto the land. For me, the tide met the land at 7 p.m. every Wednesday in a very nice sitting room in London Fields, in between the tea and biscuits and the breathing exercises. And the toilet where I would frequently need to go, not to pee but to blink until my eyes stopped watering. The loneliness of the long-distance runner has nothing on the loneliness of the single person in an antenatal class.

So imagine my delight when, about halfway through the course, one of the dads took offence at being told he should probably give up smoking before his baby was born, and he never returned to the meetings to be hectored again. To my absolute joy, the numbers balanced out fine after that.

19

A whole new world in Piss Alley

A house came up for rent on a little street nearby called Gould Terrace, and it seemed fated, too good to be true – a whole house, with an upstairs and a downstairs, on a quiet little dead end named after the pianist who had made my baby kick! Well, possibly. I had only lived in flats for the past fifteen years, so the idea of having my baby in a house – and I did intend to literally have my baby in the house, I'd probably give birth somewhere near the fireplace, but not so near that the birthing pool would catch fire – was a dream come true. The house had one room downstairs, with a kitchen area and a sitting-room area, and a bathroom with a washing machine area leading off it, and a tiny little patio with room for a hoiked-up washing line and a bench where you could sit and inhale some of East London's less aggressive pollution, because there was a house three doors down that had managed to plant a tree. The rent was going to eat up pretty much my entire monthly budget, but that was fine because me and this thing weren't going anywhere, and I'd only have to scavenge food for one person and then the baby would just eat me. The budget came, in part, from the Musician, who was doing really well in his own work, and had agreed to help financially.

In the open-plan room was a staircase, which had no kind of banister around it whatsoever, prompting a vague worry about child safety, but I let it go. Upstairs there were two bedrooms, one of which would fit a double bed. There was stained glass on the wonky bedroom doors and I was in love. It was like a cottage in the city, tucked as it was right behind a jerk chicken takeaway, a kebab shop, McDonald's, and Greggs, so, the four main food groups. I would do anything to get this house, even if it involved ramping up the lies about my husband and my employment status. The Musician and I seemed to be enjoying some kind of detente ever since our child had responded so forcefully to his choice of music, and he was paying this maintenance money monthly now, even before I had given birth. It gave me a solid sense of security to know that, between that and my own bits of income, we wouldn't have to sleep on a sofa again.

And so, after telling so many lies that my friends were hysterical when they found out, I got it. They were hysterical because I was giving the estate agents their work email addresses and phone numbers so they could pretend to be my employers and former landlords. One friend in particular was very keen on this plan, saying she would do anything to help me and that I should use her name however I saw fit, if it helped. She was the most successful person I knew, and I was convinced it would.

Which is why I ended up having to deal with a call from the estate agent saying that they'd rung *The Times* general switchboard to check, and was informed that my friend was not in fact the editor of the newspaper, but actually a columnist who worked from her home in Crouch End and therefore not legally my employer at all. Reader, I don't even remember how I got through that one – I have blanked out the memory of which even greater lie came next, because as far as houses of cards went, I was like Dolly Parton in her belief that the higher the hair, the closer to God. I just kept adding to it. As for my husband with a different surname, and who appeared to be resident in a different country, I made him send me scans of his passport and got through that one as well, what with his heavy touring schedule that only made it *appear* as if we had lived separately in different countries from each other all these years. Of course we shared a home! Somewhere.

My friends were beside themselves. 'I bet you sent them his bloody Wikipedia page and all,' said Diane, making herself chuckle. I just sat there. She looked at me. 'Oh Sophie,' she said. 'Christ.'

Well, all I can say is, it worked. My long-suffering parents lent me the deposit money, with their sighs being exhaled two hundred miles away in Yorkshire and thus rendering them just out of earshot. The agents rented me the house and I was home! We were going to build a life here, me and the baby. I moved in with my suitcases and found a cluster of light switches downstairs, none of which seemed to turn on the main light. It must have been broken, but rather than face ever speaking to the agency again, and having them come round and find there was no sign of my husband's existence or of me having a normal job, or whatever else I couldn't even remember saying to them, I simply grew accustomed to sitting in the dark.

What I didn't know, at this point, was that Gould Terrace had another name. It wasn't a name that I ever heard anyone say out loud, but it was one that became quite real to me, and uttered itself quite loudly in my mind every time I walked down the tiny street that was barely big enough for a pavement. It was Piss Alley and it was well deserved.

Piss Alley was tucked behind a heady little street called the Narrow Way, which was on its way to being pedestrianised, except for a few buses and delivery vans taking endless plastic containers to its pound shops. The Narrow Way was a vortex of psychodrama, lust, aggression and chicken nuggets. Congregating there were a lot of teenagers, street drinkers, street shouters, street dwellers, who'd been forgotten most of their lives and were trying to matter now, all of them merging into the other people trying to do their shopping with change from a tenner.

The Narrow Way was paranoid and it was also jubilant; a place where the poignant London expression, 'chat shit, get banged', meaning 'speak ill of someone and you may meet with retribution of a somewhat violent nature', really came alive, about fourteen times a day. When I was heavily pregnant a man came at me there with an aerosol, trying to spray something into my eyes. I screamed and staggered away, at which point a nice old West Indian lady approached me – I thought she was going to ask if I was all right, but no, she wanted to know if I was having twins. I replied that there was only one baby in there and she looked appalled. 'Dem tell me white babies was *small*,' she said, her eyes boggling. Soon, I would push my pram past a gang of Hackney teenagers loitering outside McDonald's every day, and I would just wonder to myself when, *when* would my child be big enough to leave me alone and join them?

Oh, but I loved the Narrow Way.

And tucked behind it, almost a secret, was my street, and my little house, where every night without fail, drunk men would trundle down to piss against our front walls, and my neighbours would put up makeshift signs to ask them to stop pissing, and the drunk men would come back and piss the signs away.

I took on another credit card, and ordered myself a bed. I'd only ever bought furniture from Ikea or Argos or junk shops crammed into railway arches before, but this time I had decided, in one of my more lucid moments, that if I was going to spend the next years of my life snatching fragments of sleep without a partner to share the load of raising a baby, then I needed those fragments of sleep to be good ones. There was nothing in my house for the baby yet either – no cot or pram or anything like that – but babies were small and could sleep anywhere, I reasoned. I remembered that episode of *Friends* where

Joey tries to persuade a pregnant, single Rachel that she can move into his apartment, 'because babies are small – we can put it here, here, or here,' he motions, holding his hands about ten inches apart and finding spaces in between the furniture. I got the joke but still quietly believed that he was right. Babies didn't need all this clobber and could sleep on a blanket in a drawer – but I couldn't.

So it was that I went to Habitat on Tottenham Court Road, and found a bed that was half price but still cost more than I'd ever spent on anything. It had a beautifully simple, wooden frame, with a flash mattress, and it was king size. It was big. It would fit whoever it needed to fit in it. I had measured my new bedroom and it was also going to fit in there, with room left to swing a cat around it. Cat-swinging being the only activity on the horizon as my social capital depleted and my social life fell apart and nobody else actually needed to fit into the bed, surely. Nobody tall, anyway.

A couple of weeks later the delivery lorry turned up, and I waited in excitement for the men to bring my brand-new bed up the stairs – I had specified that there were stairs – and for them to leave again, so I could finally put away the Tesco's camp bed I'd been using and lie down and really rest for what felt like the first time in this entire pregnancy. I was eight months gone now, and had taken about three deep breaths in the past year. It was time to admit that I was tired.

Only, when I answered the bell to them, and asked if they were going to be okay getting it through my rather small front door, the nice Glaswegian man said, ah, no problem pet, it comes in a flatpack. And he pulled all these enormous lengths of wood, wrapped in plastic, out of the back of the van, and then lugged a massive mattress up the stairs after them. I was confused – hadn't I paid all of this money so that, for the first time in my adult life, something would actually arrive fully built? So that I wouldn't have to sit there with a screwdriver like I'd been doing for fifteen years? We stood there, the man and I, surveying the pile of slabs and six-foot slats on my bedroom floor. This total stranger, who knew nothing about my life, took one look at my face and said to me, with a good heart, 'Don't worry, pet, your husband will sort all this when he gets home from work!' My head moved in some kind of nodding direction. He and the driver left, shutting the front door behind them. I remained standing there with a blank expression, while the sobs came quietly, and the kindness of his words burned a hole through my heart.

20

Orgasmic Birth: the dream

Diane came to an appointment at the hospital with me. There was a nutrition poster in the hallway and as we waited outside the room she glanced at it and then asked if I'd gone vegan yet, 'because I know two people who've had babies in the past two years and they both went bloody vegan.' I pointed out that I'd been vegan about fifteen years ago, back when I lived in that hippy Quaker commune in Bethnal Green I'd been in when she first met me. Diane was nothing like Lily – in fact, it was important that my two best friends never even crossed paths, such was the difference between them, so the continental landmass that also separated them really helped – and she loved taking the piss out of me at any opportunity.

Diane was Bethnal Green born and raised, a proper cockney, whereas all seventeen of us ponces who'd moved into the commune near her childhood block of flats were like amateur anthropologists every time we peered in the windows of the pie and mash shop. The commune had been on Bethnal Green Road itself, the very same street where Diane and her mum used to take their nan to Woolworths in her wheelchair because it made it easier for shoplifting purposes, as you could hide the bags of pick'n'mix in the wheelchair. My friendship with Diane was deeply improbable on many levels, but it was also more solid to us than the concept of God. And I was quite into God at times, and she was a Catholic.

'Oh, Jesus Christ, the *commune*,' she said, remembering, rolling her eyes with glee. 'So you aren't going to do it again because, what, you need more calories for the baby?'

'Calories?' I replied, 'God no, I was the biggest I've ever been when I was a vegan. I lived on chips and Stella. Well, mung beans and chips and Stella.' No, I didn't think I was at much risk of wasting away, I just didn't want to go down the road of obsessiveness, or focusing on all this purity stuff, or making lists of things I couldn't have ever again. I had grown up vegetarian but even that didn't appeal to me any more, even though I wasn't wildly keen on meat either. I'd just had enough of being morally righteous in any direction to last a lifetime.

'Tell me again about that guy who came to the commune,' she said, and I knew she meant Jani. 'Fuck's sake, not *here*, Di,' I replied, because we were in a doctor's waiting room, and then she did her big panda eyes and begged me and I couldn't take it any more, I was almost hysterical at the thought, so I said all right. Nobody seemed to be anywhere near us. I told her, again, about this guy who turned up at the commune unexpectedly one cold night. He was dropping in on a friend who lived there, but our eyes met and I thought he was just beautiful.

He had the loveliest bone structure I had ever seen on a man, and such a kind expression too. Jani was great.

So I was fascinated to discover, when we got talking, that he was a chef who had been living in a Hare Krishna community for the past year. The vegetarian cookery had interested him first of all, but then he'd started to study the lifestyle and had felt the religious calling – he'd actually been on his way to becoming a monk. I couldn't believe it. He was out of that scene now, had realised he couldn't go through with it, but he'd only had a month or two back in the normal world, and was still trying to process everything, and grow his hair back. It was a bit of a thing in 1990s central London, the Hare Krishna movement – you'd see them in their orange robes, shaved heads and even bare feet, all marching down Oxford Street together, playing bells and drums and happy chanting, while people walked past them laden with shopping bags from Top Shop and Selfridges. It was a sight we had all got used to, somewhere in that late nineties haze where consumerism met spirituality, but I'd never met anyone who had actually joined them.

We got on like a house on fire, me and Jani and his monastic cheekbones, and so he turned up back at the house a few nights later. Not to see his friend, but to continue his conversation with me. We ended up in my bedroom, with a certain mood in the air, where he revealed that he had also been on a vow of celibacy during his Hare Krishna year. Not even wanking? I had joked. Not even wanking, he had replied, quite seriously. If we were going to do stuff together, he explained, he just wanted to say that it had been, for him, quite some time. This was entirely new territory for me, a beautiful man being so thoughtful, so vulnerable, and I was quite moved by his emotional honesty. By his willingness to discuss the possibility of us touching each other rather than just getting drunk and making a grab for it. So I honoured his dignity with the sensitive response it deserved, the only way I knew how, which meant that I put his penis in my mouth and sucked it until he came.

Which he did really quite quickly, after making a few gasps, and when it happened, I tasted something so rank and so disgusting that it still boggles my mind that I swallowed it. What I tasted was the sperm of a man who has been eating clean and thinking beauty and trying so hard to be pure that his sperm has basically got into a backlog and turned to poison. Imprisoned poison. There was so much of the stuff, shooting out into my mouth, and it was *rancid*. It was even worse than Morning After Eight Pints of Stella Spunk, and I had tasted that particular parfum more than once. Some people used to refer to male masturbation as 'making the bald man cry', but I realised then that, for an entire year, Jani had just been a bald man, crying.

You may think, if you chance upon any members of that particular religious group, and you see their simple orange robes, those humbly bare feet, and hear their beautiful chanting of the Maha Mantra, that this is enlightenment. A higher way of being. Personally, I think it is the exact opposite. It is unenlightenment, because human bodies were designed to keep warm by rubbing up against each other, enforced chastity is a controlling myth, and the orange monks would all be a lot happier about living in this evil world if they just liquidated the inventory once in a while.

Diane, of course, was pissing herself. Absolutely wetting herself with glee at this story – again. Although she then hit on a new angle she hadn't thought of before, which was that, what if Jani was just *pretending* to have been a monk, 'Cos he'd read that book, what was it called, *Men are from Mars, Women are from Venus*, wasn't that written by someone who found out all about sex by telling women he'd been a monk?' I thought about it. Christ, I think I'd even had that book on my bedroom shelves at the exact time I met Jani.

Diane was right – it was written by a man who reckoned he had found out what women actually wanted in bed by going round asking all of them, and then doing it to them. Somehow, though, as a woman you still ended up reading the book to find out what men wanted, and then giving that to them, as if your desiring end of the bargain was far less important, and as if all men were the same, their desires and bodies the same.

It was one of several such books that I read in early adulthood, thinking that I was now so aware, so well informed, when actually they were taking me further from my own desire, my own love, than ever before. Things like *He's Just Not That Into You*, which from the title onwards made quite clear that your desires came secondary, that your job was to make yourself more chooseable, more fuckable, more wantable by a man. To play harder to get so that they could eventually feel they had won something

134

by getting you. Your verbs were passive, his were active, and one size fitted all. Titles like that affected you: seeing them every day on the shelves, they served to remind you that you were not loved, that you did not matter, and that his feelings did.

The Rules was the other big one, and yes, we all read it, memorising the strict advice that if a man asks you out after Wednesday, you have to say you're busy on Saturday, even if your diary is as empty as a bucket and you'd like nothing more but to hang out with this warm person, having a laugh. We learned to make ourselves sound unavailable, uninterested, and dishonest, to take us as far away from our instincts and big warm hearts as possible, to make the men salivate over us as bounty, as jewels, like we were money to be spent. I had felt conflicted about all this advice, but also believed, on some level, that it was all true and that these were the sacrifices we had to make in a man's world.

I had had such nice boyfriends at school and sixth form college in Yorkshire. Funny, brainy, passionate boys who I got into new kinds of art and music alongside. Boys with whom I hung out on farms, being mischievous down by the river, singing along and staying out too late scrambling up the grassy banks of our town's old medieval walls to pick illicit daffodils. There had been sex and drugs too, of course. But those boys were all right. Those boys were interested in the world and all of its colours, open to it. But then I moved to London and felt I had to be serious, because the 1990s media had announced there to be such a divide between men and women, and since I'd been battling my own divide between Sophie and the Man Behind My Eyebrows for so many years, I felt it was of the utmost importance that I get behind this new division. Show which side I was on. Fast. So whatever truth my heart had held was gone again – and then there was the drinking.

Back in Homerton Hospital, the doctor called me into the room. I left Diane outside and went in to see the consultant, because my pregnancy was now full term and absolutely nothing was happening, hence this appointment. 'I'm going to book you in for a sweep,' he said, 'which means a midwife will insert her fingers into your vagina to try to get things going in there, induce labour.' Would my sex life ever recover, I wondered, while contemplating if I should get dressed up specially for the sweep. Perhaps I should put on a Wonderbra.

Of course, my plan was to have a deeply orgasmic time during childbirth itself, having read a book called *Orgasmic Birth*, which had been recommended by a friend in California. Most British women, including me, have heard repeatedly that childbirth is going to be about as orgasmic as a punch in the fanny followed by a punch in the tits, and with the underlying suggestion that we should be *grateful* for that, because in the olden days it would have been a punch in the fanny and in the tits and then a lingering death in the mud alongside some poultry.

The orgasmic book is based on the idea that it's not just sex that gets a baby into a woman's body, but a similar sort of sexual stimulation that gets it out again, thanks to the hormone oxytocin. Nipples are to be caressed, the clitoris should be stimulated, and the whole damn game should start itself up again, easing your body through labour, and then you won't need any drugs. This is the theory. I also ordered the corresponding *Orgasmic Birth* DVD, on import from the West Coast, which showed couples and sometimes entire families delivering a child into a birthing pool in a wooden shack somewhere in a redwood forest, with the requisite number of dream-catchers and motivational quotes and culturally appropri-ated Native American feathers dangling from the rafters. I heard their groans and their grunts. I saw their lovely babies slide out like wet rags. I suspended my disbelief and thought that I could do this too.

The thing is, though, that orgasmic birth probably works best if you are on some kind of sex continuum with the person who started it, and if the sex that got the baby in there has *not* become the biggest source of conten-tion in your life. Yes, the Musician and I had reached a sort of compromise state of cooperation by this point, but his acceptance of having put the baby in there did not mean he was offering to get back in and finish the job off. Which meant I would have to do it.

With hindsight, I can say that I am now not entirely convinced that trying to induce labour by having sex *with oneself* is a winner. Especially if one is having sex with oneself, not in a Californian hot tub surrounded by dream-catchers hanging from the redwood trees, but in a window-less NHS lavatory surrounded by signs telling you not to flush used sanitary towels down the loo, which is where I ended up trying to have my baby. Especially if you've gone so far overdue that your family have been begging you to let the doctors induce you, and that eighteen days after your due date the doctors themselves have practically been on the verge of sectioning you, and that you are now on that labour ward having been given so many pessaries, drugs, injections and threats of surgery that your labour has gone about as far from nature as it is possible to get without genetically modifying yourself.

21

Unorgasmic Birth: the reality

I personally didn't believe that my baby was ready to come out, despite having been in there for something approaching a year by this point – no, I believed she would come when she was ready. This belief was brought to me not by the decades of medical experience that most people who spoke to me possessed – midwives, consultants, obstetricians – all telling me that they would like to induce my labour as soon as possible as the baby might seem to be all right in there but the placenta would decline rapidly in its vitality and ability to nourish her from now onwards. Meaning she would die.

No, my unshakeable belief in the spotless sunshine of the eternal pregnancy was brought to me by my recent joining of a Facebook group called Ten Month Mamas, which was set up by some random women in some random part of America who went overdue and didn't want to do a damn thing about it. They were opposed to medical intervention, and in a country where such intervention could be very expensive and perhaps advised for the wrong reasons (Caesareans being less likely than vaginal deliveries to lead to litigation, for example.) These women said that all the faffing of doctors and overmedicalisation of labour was a con, that giving pregnancy a specific perfect and exact duration length was a myth, and that our children would come out when they were ready, in tune with the great bingo-bango of the universal cosmos of peace and babytude and placentas that last for ever etc.

How the group worked was that somebody would write on the group wall, some total stranger to all the rest of us, no doubt, with us knowing nothing about her medical history etc. – or if she was even for real and not some kind of troll – that she had just come back from a hospital appointment where they tried to induce labour because she was at forty-four weeks and the scan revealed the placenta was calcifying, yadda yadda yadda, but that she knew this to be BIG PHARMA LIES and so she had told the docs where to stick it and had come home to let that baby carry on shooting the breeze in there. Because her baby would come out when it was good and ready and not when the doctors said it had to. And then everybody else in the group would write 'YAY WELL DONE GO BIG MAMA, good work resisting the man, you go girl-friend, HURRRRRAH!' And we would all cheer the work of the wise and go back to nurturing our birthless babies for ever.

It is interesting, now, when people talk about instincts. Just go with your *gut*, they say – your gut is never wrong! I had spent the whole of the 1990s and 2000s and beyond being told, by all the wise women of the age, to learn to listen to my gut, and so I did, even though my gut was currently being squashed by my foetus. I'd read enough of those *Eat Pray Love* type books where women learned to trust their feminine intuition, and knew it was the right thing to do in my newly feminine situation: to go along with the feminine mystique that I thought I probably now had. Possibly. I mean, my tits were definitely bigger.

So it is a real shame that my feminine intuition turned out to be such utter bollocks.

My pregnancy finished its requisite nine months and went well into the tenth. In fact, it was more than halfway to month eleven by the time I capitulated to the begging and pleading of literally everybody I knew, apart from Rebecca, my doula (a very experienced friend of a friend whom I had asked to support me in giving birth), that all hopes for a homebirth were off.

I had to be given induction drugs in the hospital and then try desperately to get my contractions going, with the threat of a Caesarean if I couldn't. Lily accompanied me, working in tandem with Rebecca – they ended up doing it in shifts because I was in the hospital for so long. Diane was also in the area nearby, though her job was largely to keep my mother occupied so she didn't storm the hospital that I had banned her from attending. This didn't stop my mother, when I was in labour, from finding out the mobile phone number of my midwife and ringing it to find out how far along I was, her frequent contact from Lily and Rebecca not proving frequent enough.

But this is why, after having some lovely pessaries inserted to chemically induce labour, I marched off down the road with Lily to try to get this labour going any way we could. I knew that lying on your back was the absolute worst thing you could do, even though they don't really tell you that in the hospital, and so we got permission to go for a walk around the hospital grounds. What we did not get permission to do was to leave the hospital altogether, walk down the road to Chatsworth Road and do some shopping at the deli, but I really wanted some juice and there was nothing much on offer in the hospital.

So off we waddled, Lily and I, me with the pessaries in action, physically inducing labour as we waddled. At the deli halfway down the long street we bought a few things, and as I paid for them at the till, the very friendly Brazilian man looked at the giantness of my bump and said, laughing, 'When is the baby due?' 'NOW,' I replied, menacingly. I wasn't in the mood by this point. 'Now?' he said, looking a little worried. 'RIGHT NOW,' I said. I was done with funny chats about this baby by this point. He became so visibly terrified of me in front of my eyes that he said I could have a free canvas bag, which I quite liked actually, and so this cheered me up a bit. I still have it. Every time I put my shopping in it, it reminds me of that lovely feeling of dinoprostone stimulating my insides until I could pop.

Anyway, I was in the Vivienne Westwood snake dress, of course, which is perhaps why I looked so additionally terrifying. Back at the hospital, where we pretended not to have just been shopping, they had a look and it didn't seem like much was going on. I was determined, and indeed desperate, to beat this system and get that baby out without any further medical intervention, and so they agreed that Lily and I could go for another walk around the grounds, but that this time, if I really wanted to get things going, perhaps I should walk up and down the stairs a few times? Having spent a lot of my last month goose-stepping around the pavements of East London and hiking up Hampstead Heath to try and jiggle that thing out, I knew the staircase trick might not work, but I had the pessaries in now and was determined to try. So determined, in fact, that after going up and down them with Lily a few times, and then up again, we decided to take a look at what happened if we went up and up past the point it said you were allowed to.

I mean a NO ENTRY sign is a red rag to a bull like me at the best of times, but to me in a snake dress while, technically, in labour, on a countdown to avoid an enforced surgery, it was too much. So we went through it, the No Entry bit, and after opening a few doors that we most definitely shouldn't have, we found ourselves on the roof. Here, while jumping around still trying to get the baby out, in the freakish bright sunlight heatwave that England enjoyed in late September 2011, we did the only natural thing we could possibly have done at this point – we staged a photo shoot. Lily got her phone out, I posed in a variety of Trying To Give Birth On A Hospital Roof In My Vivienne Westwood Dress With A Massive Snake On The Front shots. Lily sent them to friends who were desperate to hear if I'd had the baby yet. They were, it transpired, slightly surprised to see a photo of me in sunglasses on the hospital roof. But not wildly.

22

Labour wards are just like nightclubs, really

When you shove a pill down your throat in a nightclub in Manchester in 1996 in pursuit of having an absolutely lovely night out, somebody should really warn you about the consequences. I don't mean the comedown the next day, or the existential weepiness as your serotonin plunges two days after that, or the long-term risks that ecstasy might pose to your CD collection. All of that was known to me already and I still knocked it back with an alcopops chaser. No, I mean they should tell you that one day, about fifteen years later, when you're on your second day of labour in a London hospital, grunting and grinding to get your cervix fully dilated so you can push a baby out through your vagina and avoid the doctor's mutterings about it having to come out through the sunroof, and knowing that, either way, you're only hours from becoming a mother – well, they should warn you that you just might have a full-body flashback to that particular night at Sankeys Soap, when house music filled your brain and the taste of strangers filled your tongue.

The synthetic contractions are pounding your body into repetitive beats, and swaying your mind into an altered state in this hospital, which is a strange zone of industrialised intimacy, where the boundary between public and private disintegrates. There are tunes coming out of your phone. What time is love. How dilated are you now. How many centimetres is it. It's 3 a.m. eternal. Can you handle this. We might have to take it to surgery. Take it to the bridge. Your love is taking me higher. And it's busy in this room, doctors changing shifts, students peering in, strangers coming in and out and touching you, asking what you've taken, checking your BPM and writing it down on their clipboards while you writhe your pelvis around in time to the pain. This is a vibe you've only ever known in one other place and time before. It's not just a rave – it's that specific *moment* of the rave when things get weird.

The vivid flashback itself, though, comes after you ask to be unstrapped from the heart monitors so you can shuffle yourself into the loo, which is technically a wet room; a white tiled cell with a toilet and a shower in it. It has no windows, no air and no natural light, and the thought of locking yourself in there makes you feel sick, but you've been sick for hours anyway so what's new, and so you lock yourself in there anyway because you know what you have to do, and it's something you can't do in front of the doctors. This is private. Despite a day and a half of their interventions, with you half naked on

145

the bed, with their rods to break your waters and pessaries to break your jail, your cervix will still not release its captive, and it has become clear to you that now is the time to take a leaf out of the *Orgasmic Birth* book and get this party started in a way that, it appears, the drugs cannot. But you're on a lot of drugs now, is the thing. You're confused.

You're also naked, you've turned the shower on and the hot water pours all over you. Your hair is soaking, skin is perfectly burning hot and it's already taking your mind off the pain. You touch your breasts, you touch your bump, you touch yourself in all the places beyond it that you can barely even reach, now that your body is bigger than noise. You are animal, you are growls, roars, nipples, clitoris; this thing is pounding inside of you until it rises up in you and – wait. Hang on, what – there's a disturbance in the force. Your mind is thrown into a different place, a different room a bit like this one. A tiled courtyard perhaps. A lavatory.

Suddenly you aren't having a baby in this windowless cell at all. You're down by the Rochdale canal on the outskirts of Manchester in the late twentieth century, not the twenty-first, down past the industrial estates and the disused mills, in an old warehouse nightclub that is encircled by bouncers making sure nobody has brought a gun. You're with your friend who studies there, and all her friends and a load of people you've never seen before, with house music filling the air like sinister love, the piano breaks making you all cheer, the vocals rubbing you up the right way as you come up on that pill, everybody's arms floating up into the air and their inhibitions slipping down through the concrete floor and into the earth beneath, off out into the dirty canal water, to ride away like industry did.

You feel the earth like you feel the sky; as part of you, as part of everyone. And you're turning around and kissing a man you've never seen before, and the man is so beautiful and his smile so gentle and his bones so endless, that you kiss him hard and he is startled, he is delighted, and he kisses you back, deep – so deeply that you think you're going to come. It is everything and it is nothing and it is right. It is wrong. They're calling your name next door. You can't breathe in here. You're soaking wet. How long have you been in the toilet. The music isn't playing. You're grinding your teeth. Your heart is beating for two people now. But which two. Everything is closing in on you. Why isn't there any air. What time is love. They're banging on the door. They're taking this to surgery.

It's odd when people say that giving birth was the single best day of their life. Looking back on what was to happen to me after that, I can safely say that giving birth was, with literally no close competition from any other days, the absolute, hands-down, single worst day of my life. All right, the single worst *two* days of my life. My daughter is the best thing in my existence, but I can quite clearly separate loving my daughter from not enjoying ten different doctors waggling their hands and their poky things up my chuff. It is not hard to distinguish between these distinct phenomena. One is love, the other is get the fuck away from me, now.

But I do think that short time on the roof, laughing in the sunshine with Lily and with my snake and the fire in my belly and the dragon in my heart, looking out over the rooftops of East London off into the City and the Thames and the whole of this heart of my country, knowing we were probably about to set off a security alarm and end up being forcibly evacuated by the fire brigade, was probably one of the best *moments* of my life. I just wish I could have given birth right there, right then, instead of what happened next. Which is that I ended up having a nightclub flashback in a toilet, and then it went to surgery.

There's also another bit of labour, just before that, which I find hard to write about. The bit where the Musician, who had been going to come, and then not going to come, then did come, somewhere around midnight, when I'd gone deep into an animal state. Or so I thought. The bit where he'd been on stage that night and was probably stoned, been hanging out backstage, had that sort of lost grin on this face, sat at the far end of the bed, too far away, and he finally stood up and I thought he was coming towards me so I reached out my arms to touch him. I needed that contact. I needed skin. But I had misread the movement and he was in fact standing up to leave the room and walk away. A cheery goodbye came from him as I lay there, contracting, the midwives and the doctors looking at me as my arms tried to find a place to fold themselves back into. I tried to surrender as best as I could but I was no longer a wild animal. The spell had been broken. I was shame.

In the operating theatre, all I remember is asking Rebecca if she came from Bromsgrove.

R: No not from Bromsgrove but it's kind of near there, a different part of the West Midlands.
ME: Because I've been to Bromsgrove, I knew a girl who lived there once, I met her on holiday and then me and my mum once drove through the town and we found her outside her school, isn't that funny, maybe you went to the same school in Bromsgrove.
R: Yes that is funny but I didn't go to school in Bromsgrove, or Birmingham, no, it's a different town just a bit further along the
ME: And I knew someone else from Bromsgrove, someone at uni, she was called Charlotte, she'd have been older than you though if you knew her from Bromsgrove
R: Yes I'm not actually from Bromsgrove, the thing about the place where my parents raised us is that it
ME: I liked Bromsgrove, the day I drove through it. I like the idea of Bromsgrove.

I probably haven't used the word Bromsgrove for the last fifteen years but I suddenly feel certain that I will be okay if I can just find a word to keep repeating, even though there is no reason to keep saying it. Bromsgrove.

They are slicing me right open. Bromsgrove. If you are ever going through major surgery while wide awake and off your tits I recommend you say it too. Nothing truly bad can ever happen to you, and this I promise, while you are saying *Bromsgrove*.

And then a baby is passed over the white curtain to me and she is my daughter, she is a broken star, a bloodied astronaut, a bloodied moon. She is a missile coming straight for me; an answer to the question that my body asked without me knowing. She is the smallest person I have ever held and the biggest thing I have ever seen. A dishcloth of a thing. A cake, a Yoda, an alien who clearly knows everything about everything. I get the distinct feeling that I will have to teach her nothing, nothing, nothing.

I cry involuntarily. It comes from me like a bark. I start singing Blueberry Hill to her, just the line about finding my thrill again and again, those being the only words I know. We are in a loop, me and the baby who is already sort of latched onto my breast, sort of able to suck. Both of us drugged, both of us under the wooze of whatever laudanum they give you these days.

(I only remember this song about three years later, when I sing it to her again and she sits bolt upright, shocked, unable to explain why she is shocked. Around this age, three years later, she also tells me what it was like being born, and clambers off her seat on the top deck of the 425 bus to mime getting squashed in the birth canal. How narrow she makes herself, holding her arms in like she's a toilet roll tube. Then it is me who is unable to explain. A year later I ask her to do it again and she has forgotten how she was born. I am sad that the magic trick has gone but glad she has forgotten. My body has forgotten too.)

Rebecca is helping me to get the baby straight onto my breast, skin to skin, both of us as bare as we can be. I wish I was in the woods, I wish I was a bear. The baby's face is lopsided, one eye more closed than the other, a big red mark across her forehead, and I don't know how to ask if that is how she is always going to look, if I will reveal a lack of love by already wanting her to be different at twenty-eight seconds old. If I am allowed to hope that she doesn't stay like that.

She and I lie on a stretcher on wheels and some time later we are wheeled along the corridor to meet her father, and as we arrive at him I feel an acute sense of embarrassment. And on top of the embarrassment I feel an even acuter sense that this is not how it is supposed to feel when you present a man with his baby. The baby is fine. I'm alive too. It is the narrative that I can't control, and I feel it slipping away from me. I'm a writer and I am not being allowed to write this story the way I want to, not this time.

I would not wish this feeling on my worst enemy.

For a few days after giving birth I have to stay in the hospital. I'm lying there alone in my hospital bed with my three hours old baby, who the nurses keep taking from me to put in the plastic box that is her crib beside my hospital bed, and who I keep taking out of the box and lying on my chest because that is where a tiny human who was just cut out of their mother's body should be, in my arms, where we will fall asleep together. They keep taking her out and putting her back in the plastic box in case she drowns in my tired breasts. Here in this building where there is an unseasonal end of September heatwave, and there seem to be no windows that can be opened, no natural light, and so we lie here in the plastic heat and the plastic light and we listen to the sounds of the mother in the bed next door who is on the phone all day and all night telling people that she is a strong woman, such a strong woman, and meanwhile the nurses, who actually are strong women, are unable to get her to shush, and one day her boyfriend comes to see the baby and finds the sleeping newborn there but the mother gone (maybe she needs some air in this airless prison of new demands) so he calls the police or are they social workers, some kind of kerfuffle I can't quite see from behind my drowsy curtain, but they are on the ward by the time she returns, and the Hasidic man visiting his wife in the bed opposite pretends not to see the police, or me, there with my breasts hanging out of my nightie, or the nurse telling me that it's day two now and perhaps time to think about wearing some actual clothes?

We do not talk to each other, we mothers on the Hackney recovery ward. We are not a melting pot; we are melted. But I am absolutely convinced that I now know the sounds of all the different babies so well that I would recognise my own baby's cries anywhere. And so I take the opportunity, when she is fast asleep in her enforced plastic box, of making a bid for the lavatory without her. The loo is only fifteen feet away from my bed, but I can barely walk after the surgery, and using the toilet itself is going to be interesting. So it is that I sit on it for a long time, letting my bowels fall apart.

A baby is crying on the ward, and has been crying for quite a while, which I find immensely satisfying because it masks the sound of my splattering evacuation. Until the banging on the door. 'ARE YOU IN THERE?' shouts a nurse. I briefly consider replying that it depends who she's looking for.

'Your baby is crying,' she says. And there's not a lot I can do about this, what with all the stuff falling out of my broken self, but I manage to get back together and hobble out of there eventually, only to be reprimanded for not taking my baby with me to the toilet. Later that day I will carry my baby in my arms and walk across the ward with her to go to the front desk and ask a question, and when I get there I will be reprimanded for holding my baby in my arms, which is a dangerous thing to do, apparently, as I should be wheeling her around on her plastic tray, like meals on wheels.

My introduction to being a mother involves being told off by other women, again and again. Told that I am not doing it right, that there are rules. Any sense of my own instinct goes out the window as I am continually warned to get my baby further away from my body than I want her, apart from when my bowels are collapsing, when I should apparently keep her close. I want to jailbreak the pair of us out of this hospital. I want to hold my baby close to my body day and night. Get me away from where there is no plant life, no windows, no view. When I do get home, it only takes me a couple of weeks to recover from the surgery, but it takes me about a year to recover from the few days in hospital when I was supposed to be recovering, and to regain the caring instincts to protect this tiny creature, the ones that were crushed before they had even dared to begin.

23

Suddenly, I am someone's mother, oh God, is this *love*?

I t is eleven o'clock at night and the baby is small, so small. Sometimes I think she is getting smaller and it is the sound that is getting bigger. She is screaming, and her screams are filling all the rooms in my head, and my arms and legs are so much longer and stronger than hers, and yet they can do nothing to stop the screaming. They are stupid limbs; appendages to my stupid body. The baby is not stupid, she is clearly screaming because she knows everything, and everything is wrong, and I do not know how to make it right.

The door to my bedroom opens and my dad walks in. My parents have moved into my house for the first eight weeks of my daughter's life, to help. It is my mother who knows how to do most things, how to raise a baby, and who has already done so much for us, and paid for much of it too. But she is asleep on a blow-up mattress downstairs and it is my father who comes in now. He sees that the baby is not the only one crying, because I am now on the carpet with her, crying too. He takes one look at us together and I feel myself caught in his gaze, like shame in amber. Found out. Until he says, in his soft, steady way, nodding like a toy dog, 'This is how it is.' And then I am a child at home again in my sobbing.

'Would you like me to take her outside in her pram and wheel her around until she falls asleep?' he says. It is late at night, pitch black outside, November, Piss Alley, and my dad, who is not from round here, and has never lived here, is about to turn eighty.

'Yes,' I whimper.

'You get into bed,' he says, as I start dressing the baby up in layers of warm clothes for her big night out. 'I'll do this, Soph, you go to sleep.'

And so I climb into my big empty bed and burrow down in it, drown in its comfort. I pass out almost instantly. I don't know when I last felt safe in bed, or slept a whole night through. Moments later, I sit bolt upright. Oh my God, her hat. He will have put it on her, won't he? He will have seen it downstairs, he will have put it on her, and snuggled her in her pram and taken her outside in her woollens and coat. He won't have taken a baby outside on a cold night without her hat.

I tell myself this and try to go back to sleep, but it's no good. I'm wide awake now.

He won't have known about the hat.

It doesn't even matter about the hat.

The hat is not necessary.

156

The hat is just more stuff.

It does matter about the hat.

I get out of my warm bed. I creep downstairs and there I see it, on a table. I go back upstairs to get dressed, then I put on my own coat, go out into the freezing nearby streets and walk around on my own until I find them, a few streets away. 'I forgot to give you her hat,' I tell him, and we both apologise, to whom I'm not sure. We get it onto her, even though she is nodding off now, calmed by the cold air going into her angry lungs, and I go back to my house and something grips me in the guts of me, the deep of me. It is a cold, hard fact. And this is it, and it is true: that wherever I go, now, for the rest of my life, and whatever I do, and whatever freedoms I am granted, I am always going to be worried about whether my daughter is cold, and whether she is wearing her hat. And that I will never be able to give this feeling back.

My parents moved out eventually, and when I think back to those first few months when my human milk still flowed, it's the night feeds I remember. In the early hours of the night, stillness would descend, the baby would wake me and I'd plug her onto my body and sit there in the dark, in my moonlit bedroom. The tube line that ran underneath my house and the overground railway line that ran beside it would both have stopped rumbling and rattling, no more trains whizzing along to Hampstead Heath and on to Richmond, all those storybook places with their trees and hills and rivers and large gardens and Poggenpohl kitchens. I could forget about them and instead turn on the false moon that was my iPhone, and the baby and I would listen to Drake, rapping so sweetly about all the bitches he knew and how it was late at night but he should probably call one of them and get his dick sucked. Oh babe.

The Portuguese have a word, the *madrugada*, to describe those hours between midnight and dawn, that delinquent part of the night that has yet to admit that it is the morning. It reminds me of Tommy Cooper, who used to do a joke where he rang up and said, 'Is that the local swimming baths?' and the voice replied, 'It depends where you're calling from.' I had always been a night owl not a morning person, ever since I was a teenager and started going to parties. The *madrugada* had always contained my finest hours, and I'd made my home in its great dark beautiful nothing while the rest of the world was sleeping. A club kid. And now I was back in it again, only this time I was alone, sober, with a warm body of pure need attached to my body and her father already gone. It would all come to me in these hours – were they late, were they early? I didn't know if the *madrugada* was where my day began or where it ended. The seams of time were split wide open. I was no longer sure where I was calling from.

So I'd tune into Drake, who didn't seem entirely certain where he was calling from either. He'd be singing in a droney monotone about these girls who should reply to his texts more quickly. How he's the only Canadian rapper who made it big and bought his mum a house and now she's lonely on the rich side of town. How he doesn't feel enough of his feelings. His late-night ennui would seep out of my phone and I'd be able to feel just the right amount of mine: a regulated amount of sadness; a slick, corporate release of pain. Because everyone talks about a baby bringing new life, but less about the grief this creates in you, when part of you, your old life, has to die to create it.

And as the baby would suck, my hormones would release a dart of serotonin and then I'd feel these surges of love towards her. Great chemical rushes of the stuff! Ahh, love! Because babies are love, and babies are sorrow, and there is something about the night feed when both those feelings want to make themselves known so very strongly. And until you accept that motherhood is both, you will become your own personal Narrow Way, full of psychodrama and paranoia and spilt beer.

24

Suddenly, that's the health visitor again, oh God, *hide*

Of course there was another reason for me to enjoy the night feeds, which is that it was the only time of day it was truly safe for me to look out of my window. You see, shortly after the birth of the baby I'd been issued a health visitor who walked in coughing on her first visit, examined the baby while still spluttering all over her, said not to worry it was just allergies, and proceeded to ask me a list of questions from her clipboard without stopping to hear my answers.

HEALTH VISITOR: Does Mum smoke?
(What you soon learn from NHS professionals is that when they say the word 'Mum', they are actually talking about you, but childbirth apparently strips you of your name. I hadn't smoked for a year by this point, having given up my occasional fags as soon as I found out I was pregnant, so I said no.)

ME: No.

HEALTH VISITOR: Does Dad smoke?

ME: Well, actually, yes he does a bit, but the thing is he doesn't live in this house so it doesn't make much difference.

HEALTH VISITOR: So that's a yes.

(She ticked a big red danger box on her form, with some satisfaction.)

ME: No, because he doesn't even live in this house.

HEALTH VISITOR: The smoke can still be on his clothes!

(And then I lost it.)

ME: He doesn't even live in this *country*, the baby was an accident, I mean he even got a new girlfriend when I was pregnant, he's really not here, we were never married, and they're in Europe and he's probably with her now and he was there at the birth but only *sort* of and he's been to visit a couple of times but you know not really much, never changed a nappy, not like that. I swear to you there isn't any smoke anywhere near the baby *at all*.

'OH!' replied my heath visitor, finally looking up from her clipboard to look at me. '*A single mother!* I'll put you on the watchlist for post-natal depression then!'

Tick.

The next time she came round, the real blessing was that I wasn't in. She left messages. She came again when

161

I *was* in, but I got wise to it, and the minute I heard wheezing in my porch I would duck down behind the sofa and will the baby to stay silent until the health visitor had gone. The woman would keep on knocking and I would keep on hiding, my heart pounding hard, crouched there all folded in on my Caesarean scar. Eventually, the health visitor stopped coming altogether.

At this point, the *Guardian* journalist in me wanted to make a fuss about this, and write a harrumphing letter of complaint, saying that if a new mother on the post-natal depression watchlist disappears from sight then the health authorities should probably do a damn sight more about it. Yet the rest of me recognised that I could not, in all good faith, write this letter because I had been hiding down the back of my sofa.

She needn't have worried anyway – the baby was getting plenty of stimulation in our new life on the Narrow Way, exposed to all the fabulous local sights and smells. Well, mainly smells – and what a choice of them we had. Should you want the baby's Proustian madeleine to be the essence of diesel from the exhaust pipes of idling number 55s, I rocked her to sleep downwind of the bus depot, where red double-deckers trundled in and out all day, huddling together for warmth when they parked there at night. Should I be more sleep-deprived myself and require baby's nap to be of a higher impact, why not try a trip to the Vietnamese nail bar, where just a few whiffs of the pink shellac poison that is being applied to my toes will seep through her blanket into those baby nostrils and send her dozing? Or stand outside St

Augustine's Tower, the only remnant of a church first built in the thirteenth century, where Henry the Eighth's right-hand-man Thomas Cromwell used to worship but only the tower and a patch of grass now remain. Its clock was once the only way for the residents of Hackney to tell the time, which is ironic, because it is now surrounded by people making the time go away entirely by drinking Special Brew from dawn till dusk, arguing among them about who told which lie about who to whom, while their dogs urinate on the discarded bones of takeaway chicken. So not all that different from the court of Henry the Eighth.

Then there is the stench of piss and promises from all three betting shops. Or the exotic whiffs from the customers of the dealers on the corner of Pembroke Road, who've relocated here from Murder Mile to sell the drugs that cause this area to be fondly known as Crackney. Then there's Greggs, which pumps out the aroma of beef and onion pasties, and the Asian grocer's with its heady fragrance of jackfruit. In a few years, the enormous jackfruit will be seized by hipster vegans as the magic ingredient to fill their tacos, when they discover that, if you cook the national fruit of Bangladesh for more than an hour, it tastes mysteriously like pulled pork. But for now, white people merely walk past and gawp at how something so big and so spiky could ever grow on a tree. And then, last but not least, there are the roadworks that stink of tar, because London is a building site, riding another boom of property speculation that will send the people of the Narrow Way even further into their tins of extra-strong lager while the new flats go to foreign investors and London real estate becomes the global reserve currency.

And the foreign investors will say the flats are for their children's future as global citizens, able to move freely throughout the world, and I'm proud to think I've already given the same gift to my daughter. Just think, she will now feel equally at home with the smell of Cornish pasties, Chinese nail glue, Polish beer and crack pipes. For the rest of her life, she will feel instantly transported back to her mother's loving breast whenever she catches a whiff of a Filet o Fish, a massive spliff or a can of Special Brew. I have made her at home in all worlds.

25

Should you breastfeed on a first date?

When it happens I don't fully understand that it is happening, or what to do about it, and I panic. A live human male person, a man, is actually chatting me up at a party, and for the first time in a year I do not have a baby inside my womb, or hanging from my breast, or snoring beside me in a pram. I can pass, for all intents and purposes, as a single person. I'm even wearing a nice black dress and red lipstick and my hair is clean for the first time this century. Look at me, beaming from ear to ear because the baby is at home with my mother, and damn it feels good to fire off into the dark city night on my own. The night has always been mine, selfishly mine, indulgently mine, and I want the night back, if only for four hours. To taste the darkness of the outside world and all the powers of transformation that it offers. Just a glimpse. Just to get a shot of it in my bloodstream.

I'm at a party in Soho for my friend Charlie's birthday, which he celebrates in the same place every year, and at which Ross from *Friends* once turned up uninvited with a mutual friend, and so just in case that happens again we all come back without fail every January just casually hoping to see him again. The baby is three months old now and it is the perfect time for me to take part in that ceremonial and ancient ritual – Your First Night On The Lash After Giving Birth.

Of course, most new mothers go on a night out to have some respite from the four walls that surround them, and the feeling of being needed at every second of every day, and to see people with whom they can laugh about something other than mastitis, and while those are my goals too, I also have another motive not shared by any other new mother who I've ever met. I have come out on the pull.

I mean come on – I'd basically been in an enforced period of singledom for a good year by now. Pregnancy is not an *ideal* time to meet someone, but I'd got through that, and was now in the afterwards stage where you're merely leaking milk from your breasts through your clothes. So that was fine, I reckoned. In fact, it was more than fine – because said milk, when it was safely contained in its rightful globular containers, was making them enormous, swelling to a size they had never been before and might never be again. I'll be honest here: my breasts were obscene. They looked like a Choose Your Own adventure story that had gone rogue somewhere around Las Vegas, and it seemed almost rude to waste them on a baby. I'm a generous person. I wanted to share my newfound fortune with others. With men.

In fact, the desire to share them had been so great that at one point, when The Musician was in my house on one of his few visits to the baby, I had felt the urge to pull up my top and show them to him. We were hardly getting along easily at this point, and all intimacy between us had been long forgotten. He was fascinated by our child and how she was developing, always noticing new things about her, and seeming to marvel at them. He would want to push her in the pram, see if she fell asleep, get to know her tiny habits. But between us we were entering the ice age, both of us straining to keep this deeply rickety show on the road. Still, I felt I had to show him. So I said, while he sat on my sofa and I stood in front of him, 'You have to see my tits.' And he said, er, okay. I pulled up my dress, got them out, and his eyes nearly broke. He'd known me for years, he'd known *them* for years, but this was something else. 'Oh … my … *God*,' he said, staring. And I just put my dress back down again and said, I know I know, while nodding. His mouth opened. 'Could you just … do that again?' he asked. I mean, it would have been churlish to refuse. 'Wow,' he said, his eyes recovering as I lowered my dress back down for the second time. I think it was the single greatest conversation we had that year.

So, back to the party – there is a man trying to talk to me. He has never been on *Friends* but nor is he someone I accidentally started a family with, so there's hope. He's a real grown-up in a suit jacket, and he looks distinguished and dignified and all the other adjectives that have never applied to me. He's wearing thin-rimmed glasses that must have been expensive, because the rule is that the less frame there is, the more the frame cost. When he catches my eye and introduces himself I immediately feel the whooshing rush to my heart that can only mean one thing: total and utter inadequacy.

'What do you do?' he asks, as one does, and suddenly I'm back in the land of old me. Only, I'm not old me. I want to be her. I can't find her.

I tell him that I'm a journalist, 'but … I'm not really working at the moment.'

Which sounds bad – he's going to think nobody wants to employ me, or that I'm lazy, oh God, quick, Sophie, salvage it.

'Because I've just had a baby!' I add, hurriedly. Phew, that should fix it. Wait – why do his eyes say that it isn't fixing it at all?

I don't wish to disparage my former self, but looking back on this situation with hindsight, I can safely say that, if a man is trying to ascertain your availability, then telling him that you recently spent a year carrying another man's seed is not the *ideal* way to convince him of it. Of course I *was* available, and again, by looking into his confused eyes I was able to realise my mistake pretty quickly, and so salvage the rapidly deteriorating situation.

'But I've already split up with the dad!' I barked, solving everything.

And just in case that didn't clarify my desperately single status enough, my brain helpfully nipped back in for one killer finale.

'In fact, I actually had the baby on my own.'

I'm not suggesting that most men don't love babies. I'm just saying, again with the benefit of the rear-view window that is time itself, that perhaps this is not the sort of information one should divulge before a total stranger has had time to breathe out.

In any case, I don't get to find out what he thinks, because, oh my God, he has turned around to talk to someone else. He's gone. He's literally gone. And my whole body exhales. I go and sit at a table with some people I vaguely know, and I'm still laughing to myself, and there's a bloke beside me who doesn't look snooty or expensive, just friendly, and he asks what I'm chuckling at. I realise I already have a story with a punchline. So I retell what just happened, giggling even harder. And he laughs too, a relaxed sort of chuckle, and goes, 'So you're not with the father any more?' And I laugh and say no, no, I'm *really* not. But this time I'm not announcing it with a desperate zeal, I'm just wheezing with relief that I have got through it – that I will never again have to experience The First Time A Man Chats Me Up After Having A Baby On My Own.

It takes me a moment to realise that I'm already experiencing the second.

Man Number 2 has big open eyes, with deep lines around them that suggest he's been smiling like this for years. If he is distinguished, it is not by the shape of his glasses but by the kindness he gives off. Our mutual friend properly introduces us, explains that Robin is such an old and trusted friend of hers that she even made him godfather to her children. As we talk, it comes out that he had a long engagement that didn't end in marriage. He works in the media, like most of the people in this room, although unlike the rest of us he doesn't seem to have the ego to match. Instead, he has a smile like everything is going to be all right for ever, and it catches the part of me that suspects, deep down, that everything is going to be all right for ever too.

You must always notice, when you meet someone, which part of you is ignited by which part of them. Is it the part of that you desperately wants to show off, ignited by the part of them that seems anxious about status and money? Is it the drinking too fast and smoking too much part of you that senses a partner with whom to smash up all the things in the room and tear into your own future like a sexy velociraptor? If that is the case, then do you think that maybe, just maybe, they're not the one?

Before I know it, it's time to leave. The glass carriage is going to turn into a pumpkin; the baby is going to need feeding in the middle of the night. I leave with our friend who then gets a text asking if she's allowed to give him my number. YES, I say, when she shows me her phone. She sends it. Within a few days we have arranged that Robin will come to my house and take me out for dinner in the next few days, because this is a good week for me to go out again, this is the week when I actually have a babysitter. Which only means one thing. Oh God. Oh no. Christ no. On our very first date, Robin is going to meet my baby – and my mother.

*

So he comes to pick me up and here we are, all waiting to greet him at the front door: the three of us. (Insert emoji of gritted teeth and dread here.) Sexual relations and my actual relations are coming ominously close to overlapping. I have spent the last few years living in my own apartment on the Sunset Strip and coming home at 4 a.m., but now I have to be chaperoned on dates by my mother. My house is open plan, so there is literally nowhere to hide, and believe me I've tried. Still, he's such a nice person that he turns out to be Good With Mums – just as well as there are two of those in the room – and he tells us that he spends an awful lot of time with his own mother too.

'Yeah I go to my mum's quite a lot,' he says, 'because she's ninety and she's a widow, and she won't lock the door! She absolutely insists that she's fine, though, says she lives in a small friendly town with no danger in it, not like London. She's always saying "Honestly, what could ever happen to me in Hungerford?"' For those readers too young to remember the biggest British news event of 1987, the Hungerford Massacre, well, let's just say that my mother does and this story has rendered her hysterical with laughter. Unfortunately, the baby seems a bit triggered by laughing about mass murder, and she starts to cry. Properly, hungrily cry.

There are moments in life when I frantically scan the mental database in my head to find out what I'm supposed to do, racking my brain for an article I once read on this, the thing a friend told me to do if it happened, the episode of a TV programme where they all dealt with this. I've got nothing. The baby is three months old and she is crying because she is hungry. But she can't be, because I cleverly timed Robin's arrival to fit in with her feed, which I completed before he knocked on the door, meaning that she can now rest easy for the few hours it will take me to go to a local restaurant with him and eat. It's only been half an hour – she can't be hungry again. And yet, she continues to wail.

'I think,' says my mother, in her best must-I-deal-with-simpletons-for-the-rest-of-my-*life* voice, as we all stand staring at the crying baby, 'that she needs feeding.'

I stare a bit more. 'She doesn't,' I say. 'I fed her before Robin got here.'

'Well she needs feeding again,' replies my mother.

'She's just tired,' I say.

'She's hungry,' says my mother.

'That's her tired sort of cry,' I mutter.

Everyone is no longer staring at the baby, who is screaming even louder. They are staring at me. I feel paralysed. Like those dreams where somebody is holding you down and you can't wake up. Here's the thing: we haven't got to tits yet. He hasn't *earned* tits yet. And call me old-fashioned, but I just don't think that the first time this lovely man sees them, they should be in somebody else's mouth.

It's not as if I'm conservative by nature. My life is something that has rolled out in one big crash and has never stopped crashing, not since the day at primary school when I was so gripped in doing my jigsaw that I refused to go to the loo and instead I thought I'd pee right down my legs in my chair to save time. I'll breastfeed in front of anyone – my own brother, Nigel Farage, the bus driver, etc. And I've chosen this guy specifically because he seems so warm and supportive and understanding. Bruised by the whole experience of having a baby on my own, I have made a conscious decision that I will overhaul my own experience of love, and stop longing to have people who aren't haveable. I've made a conscious decision to wrest my own sexuality away from bad boys. I'm going for nice.

There is a poem I once read about a man who gets up for work early in the winter mornings, getting dressed quietly because his wife is still sleeping. Before he leaves the bedroom, he silently slips her second-best bra onto the radiator, so that all day at her work she will feel his hands, warm, around her. I have decided, from now on, to look at a man and ask myself not if he's dangerous and broken and if he looks like he could give me a kind of pain that is already familiar to me, but rather, if he would be the type to warm up my second-best bra.

So I stand there like frozen Arctic tundra, caught between the identity of the old me who would do anything and say anything, and the new me who hasn't yet found the words to rebuild herself with. The old me, whose body was part of the joke, and the new me, whose body is part of the solution. The new me who wants to have a respectable relationship with this respectable man, and the old me, who wants to do things my mother can't see, and the current me, who wants the ground to open up and swallow her. And who also feels, suddenly, that those occasional top-up bottles of formula milk we've resorted to giving the baby, that I've been feeling absolutely awful about, are really a *fantastic* idea and should be brought out more often.

'Do you want me to nip upstairs while you feed her?' asks Robin, and I say yes, with a gratitude bordering on the pathetic, and he goes and sits on my bed while I sit and unpeel my top in front of my mother, again. In the weeks that pass, Robin will turn out to be a real second-best bra on radiator kind of person. But it will also transpire that I can't reset my sexual attraction overnight. I am so used to being a rebel, or is it a narcissist, that I don't know how to have a partner. The irony is that my mother, who has been with my dad since she was twenty-one, is becoming my partner now. Never having wanted to build a marriage like my parents had, I now find myself in need of their help more than ever before, because the stability they offer is exactly what my baby and I require. The irony is not lost on me.

In any family where one child is the straight one and another child is the rebel, it is always the straight, well-behaved one who gets away furthest. They may not get away first, but they get away furthest, whereas the rebels always come home to roost. Rebels borrow money. Rebels borrow help. Rebels borrow love. The quietly organised person, meanwhile, with their boring spreadsheets and boring accountability, buys a flat and gets on with their life; childhood completed. It's the prodigal one, who has fled the coop, who always returns. Asking if they can have a bit more of their childhood, because they didn't finish in time.

So if you are a parent who feels you have missed out on a relationship with your more rebellious teenager, who seems to be living a secret life from you, never wanting to tell you where they go at night, then don't worry too much, because by the time they're thirty-five years old they'll probably be ringing you three times a day and you'll know whether they had tuna or cheese in their sandwich at lunch. Rebel children get enough distance when they're young, so they try to claw back the closeness when they're older, convinced that life owes them a debt of parenting which can be cashed in fifteen years on.

26

The walls are white and my eyes are red

The private clinic was as white as the *here comes the science* part of a L'Oréal advert, or as the dream sequence bit in a sitcom when the character goes to Heaven and finds angels wafting about, whitely. The walls were white, the floor was white, the staff were all dressed in lab coats that were glaringly, brilliantly white. Nobody spoke, but the room itself seemed to suggest that it could find my sins out. As I pushed the pram inside I felt a shudder every time its wheels squeaked.

We gave our names at the desk and waited to be called. There wasn't much small talk to be had between the two of us adults. The baby slept. The clock ticked. We went into the private room. The doctor seemed highly intelligent, talking us through the clinical procedure before explaining that she was legally obliged to ask us why we were having it. I'm usually quick to talk but I decided to sit this one out. And so we waited, the doctor and I, both turning to look at the Musician. I think I may, for a nano-second, have even enjoyed the look on his face.

'We just, we just want to be sure,' he said, stuttering a bit. It was an innovative usage of the first person plural, seeing as I was perfectly sure already. 'Just, you know, just for the avoidance of doubt,' he added, nodding as if everyone was already agreeing with him. I looked from him to her, and she looked from him to me, and she and I both knew that nobody in that room was agreeing with him.

'The baby doesn't have to be woken for the procedure,' she explained, 'as we can swab her mouth for the saliva sample while she's asleep in her pram. You won't even need to take the covers off her.' My relief was marred only by my disappointment that nobody would now get to see what I had dressed my four-month-old in: a grey babygro from the Myleene Klass range at Mothercare that had one word lovingly stitched across it in handwritten appliqué: *Daddy*.

The doctor swabbed each of our mouths with a separate sterile bud, which then went into sealed plastic bags on which she wrote labels that I couldn't see, but which possibly didn't say Mummy, Daddy and Baby Bear. When it was all done, and the credit card handed over, and the receipt signed with my blood, I mean his pen, he and I stood outside on the street and looked all around us. It was preferable to looking at each other.

This was when I realised that we'd been under the shadow of the Gherkin the whole time. The biggest, most phallic new skyscraper on London's skyline, only a couple of years old and bulging with guilt already. Of course, its mirrored surface was looming over our heads outside this private clinic in the City, which was the nearest place we had found that did these sort of tests. The Gherkin, it appeared to me, was a great stupid cock of a thing, and it was not alone. The baby, meanwhile, appeared to be taking the longest nap of her life, which was so unusual that I had to reach in and check that she was still breathing. She was, she just wasn't stirring. Apparently, she had simply decided to give today a miss, and who could blame her? She was a classier act than the rest of her immediate family.

And then the Musician and I tried to talk, but only revolting angry words came out. I was done with hearing those. I was done with feeling them. I was done with anything revolting even being thought near the child who I had been trying to feed with my own body for four months, even though not enough milk came, even though she sometimes still screamed after an hour on my breast, even though she was always hungry, even though we had been back to the hospital and seen four different specialists, even though she had been losing weight when she was supposed to be gaining, even though I had let endless people examine and knead and pump my breasts because I was failing in my duty as a cow. And I still felt like a cow. But a bad, failing cow. I was tired. I was so very tired.

My body was not enough for my daughter, it seemed, but I decided, there and then, to make damn sure that my mind was going to be. The Musician had visited us a few times since her birth, and he had tried, and I had tried, and sometimes I had thought that just maybe there was magic there between them – but it hadn't worked. He had asked for this private clinic DNA test, and I was done with the bullshit. This gaslighting from him. I was through. So I began to walk away, pushing the pram down the street. The shouting carried on at my back. There were threats. I pushed the baby to the end of the street, and then round the corner to the end of another street, and then suddenly I was free, surrounded by strangers bustling through the financial heart of London on their lunch breaks. What a blur they made. The City could hold me, just for a minute, while my heart pounded and gradually reworked itself into the bigger shape of things.

And then my heart stopped pounding, because I saw him coming towards me again, angry shoulders hunched and as big as Godzilla. He didn't see me though – he was shouting into his phone, furiously, something about, *and then I fucking said that*. I distinctly remember wondering if he was talking to someone who loved him.

The clinic phoned us individually a week later. The baby was his, they told me, even though the technology didn't yet exist to prove it 100 per cent, but they could give us a 99 per cent likelihood, and that was enough to take the legal burden of proof beyond the shadow of doubt, or the valley of death, or something, something, words. It was actually the very same doctor on the phone, and I could hear her hesitation at the end of the call, where professional boundaries seemed to be preventing her from asking if I was all right. I wasn't, as it happened. My milk had dried up for good the day after the paternity test, apparently due to stress. I hadn't been able to give birth to this baby naturally or give her a loving family home and now I couldn't feed her either. It just seemed rude. But what did it matter, because even though she said the baby was his, I now knew it wasn't true. That baby wasn't his, at all. She was mine, all mine, and nobody else's.

Still, the child-maintenance payments continued to come into my bank account from his, in the strange monthly mechanics of automated nothingness. Sometimes they felt like a mockery. Sometimes they felt like an apology. Sometimes they just felt like a great big help that would let me pay several bills, and it was relief. The months passed into years, and the anger turned into pain, and the pain turned into a ghost that sat on my shoulder and flicked my nerves while allowing me to live, but after that day at the clinic I didn't know if I would ever want to see him again.

27

How not to use the internet

It is often said that having a child gives your life meaning. Before having one myself I had always thought this such a strange thing to say. My own father had taught me to test the mathematical rigour of all philosophical notions quite thoroughly, and surely, the problem with this particular theory was that if you had to create a new person to give your life meaning, wouldn't that child soon enough graduate from childhood and have to create a new person to give *their* life meaning, and so on and so on? What was the point of it all? This great Jacob's Ladder of meaningless people unfolding, all needing to look to the next generation to find any point in their own? The very idea was *unmechanical*, as my father would also have said. It seemed a dereliction of duty: the responsibility to find meaning should be found within ourselves alone.

Well, I can tell you now, the theory does actually hold water, it's all true – having a child absolutely gives your life meaning. It's just that the second half of the sentence is missing, which is *but the meaning is not the child!* The meaning is everything else in your life brought into sharp relief by the simple fact that every second you spend on it is delicious and empowering and amazing simply because it is *not your fucking baby*. Seriously, even doing a shit, alone on a toilet with the door shut and enough time to wipe your arse *and* flush *and* pull your trousers up afterwards, becomes an exotic luxury akin to holidaying in a private beach resort in the Andamans with a butler and a yacht. Doing a shit becomes *very meaningful indeed*. As does flicking through a magazine. Drinking a cup of tea. Staring out of a window. Going for a walk. Working! Oh God, working, earning money, becomes the most deeply meaningful thing of all! In fact, absolutely anything that doesn't directly involve your child becomes so deeply imbued with significance and resonance that it is as if an outline has been drawn around your life with a thick black Sharpie.

But back to the shitting: if they made porn for new parents, it would feature lavatories rather than beds. Once, when my baby was about a year old, she managed to go into my bedroom while I was on the loo, come back into the bathroom right next door with a pair of my high-heeled shoes and insert them into the knickers that were around my knees while I was too busy evacuating to stop her. So there I was, not only being gawped at while I was on the loo, but juggling stilettos in my underpants while doing so. Ta. Thanks.

And yet, this was a new kind of love. Sometimes it came to me in surges, sucking my breath from my chest, or yanking my balance from beneath me like a tablecloth in a magic show. But the love, like the table, would remain. Sometimes it wounded me, getting me somewhere vulnerable while I was trying to keep a handle on things, turning me into an injured deer. Sometimes I felt like Bambi's mother and sometimes I felt like Bambi, but either way, the passion for her and the responsibility remained. This baby needed me and I gave unto her, repeatedly. This was the oldest sort of relationship and yet it was entirely new to me, like an exotic language I had heard about but never really believed I would be able to speak.

Here's the deal: a baby doesn't talk to you properly for two years – there are no thank yous, it just wants stuff constantly, and you have to give it. It can't reason with you for four years, and it can't be left alone with the scissors for six, and that's just the way it is, and you simply have to get on with it. The strange thing was, I found that I liked having my choices taken away. I liked having to do things with no discussion, no debate. I liked being needed. I had never really been this important before. No more time for indulgent and obsessive wondering about my purpose on this earth – I was a celebrity in my own home! I had tried plenty of cures for existential angst but having a baby was definitely the one.

Even if, in reality, this tended to mean going to get a baby wipe from the packet of wipes, wiping something up either on or near the baby, taking the wipe to the bin, putting the packet away again, coming back from the packet to realise something else had happened that meant another wipe was now needed, and doing it again, all while feeling deeply guilty about the wipe not being a reusable cloth that I would definitely use next time. That was basically it, repeat to fade, day or night, ceaselessly. My father had always told us that Bertrand Russell classed all human endeavour into two kinds of work: 'altering the position of matter at or near the earth's surface relative to other matter, or telling other people to do so' (yes, that was his all-time favourite quote). It was intended to explain the difference between the bourgeoisie and the proletariat, and now I felt myself becoming someone who simply moved the stuff around, having taken part in a bigger, national conversation, previously. My position in the class system and the digital age meant that, had I not become a mother, I might have avoided ever doing so otherwise.

I still worked as a journalist too, though – there's no maternity leave for a freelancer – so I wrote think pieces on my BlackBerry with one hand while nursing the baby with the other or while she slept. In public, I put on a brave and cheerful face. A friend commented that I never seemed to moan about raising a baby on my own. I didn't feel that I could – other people had surely been this close to the earth's surface for years? Maybe, I told myself, it was simply my turn to taste a bit of the work that came without glory. But it was also deep in those mind-numbingly boring repetitions of matter-moving that my love grew. I had sung along to the Massive Attack song 'Teardrop' so many times, with its line about love being a verb, a doing word. Finally I was starting to understand what it meant.

There is this other quote, though, that some parents had bandied about before I had a kid, about how becoming a parent means you cease to be the most important person in the room. Well, that had turned out to be a load of absolute balls. Having a kid makes you into the most important person, not just in the room but in the world. My daughter didn't even want anyone else to put her coat on, even though they would have done it the exact same way that Mummy did it. She wanted Mummy for everything, even if her capable and committed Granny was there, or an intriguing new visitor. Within our small world, I was Beyoncé. I was Wonder Woman. I was God. I had earned this undue level of adoration purely through repetition and proximity, but that was all right, because repetition and proximity turned out to actually *be love*. There was no other secret formula for what we had: repetition and proximity, which can be combined in the single word *familiarity*, were actually it. And, of course, if you could do all of that with *affection*, you were really onto something.

I hadn't felt it in the hospital. I don't know if it was the drugs, the fear, the sorry state of my life at that point, but when she was first handed to me, I didn't feel the rush of love that I had heard about from so many other people. Not exactly. Not love like a relief. Yes, I felt an immediate need to protect, to enclose, to guard. But love? Wanting? I don't know. In fact, it only happened when she was eight months old and doing something on the living-room floor – trying to crawl onto the armchair perhaps. I remember looking at her and suddenly realising, oh God it's *you, it's you it's you!* And exhaling with my whole body for the first time in that short lifetime.

It was when I went from coping to enjoying. It happened again, taking me to another layer of recognition of her, when she had just turned two. It's hard to explain, but I remember taking another deep breath, really looking at her again, and a deeper order of love kicking in. And so it continues now. In fact, if it goes on like this I'll be so consumed with adoration just from looking at her that I'll be getting carted off with smelling salts by the time she's ten.

But this doesn't mean that I wasn't fucking bored. Oh God, I was bored. *Christ* almighty, I was fucking bored. People visited, but I wished they would visit more. If someone said they'd come round to see the baby but then cancelled at the last minute I was gutted – that would have been my thread of hope, my one plan for the day. I was experiencing isolation of a whole new kind, and it made me long for company, which is where the internet came in. Twitter had been getting quite big during my pregnancy, and on it I was lucky enough to have become part of a gang of brilliant funny women, many of whom were journalists like me. I had known them offline too, but the daily banter of Twitter brought us much closer together. We enjoyed being rude to each other in public. It was all grist for the mill of a vibrant new feminism that was knocking down the walls that had held us in.

One day I was talking to a friend on Twitter, and I said she must come and visit me and the baby soon, and bring a mutual friend whom we shall call Sophie Bumbleson. Only what I actually said was to 'bring that slag @sophie-bumbleson with you too', which might have been funny, had I not used the wrong Twitter handle for our friend who used the abbreviation @sophbumbleson. The person I had tweeted instead, using the full form of the same name, was a total stranger. Not only that, but she was a total stranger who was fifteen years old, in hospital, and in a coma. Her Twitter account was being run by her doting father, who used it to organise fundraising for her care, and to contact her favourite celebrities to see if they would record messages to play to her in the hospital bed where she lay unresponsively.

This doting father was quite surprised, after receiving an unexpected tweet from a broadsheet journalist, that I was calling his comatose child a *slag*. I was horrified when it became clear what I had done, and tried to explain that it was an accident, but he seemed to believe that I was some loudmouthed hack who had decided to abuse his innocent girl for kicks. Things did not improve much when my Sophie, on discovering what had happened, quickly joined in the emerging online argument to stick up for me. The reason why this didn't help much is because my Sophie wrote to him that I had definitely intended the message for her, and not his daughter, 'because I really am a massive slag'.

He kept on replying to us, still using the Twitter account that bore the name and the photograph of his teenage daughter Sophie, which was of course the exact same name as the other Sophie. This would have been confusing enough on its own, but given that I'm also called Sophie, there were now three Sophies all tweeting back and forth at each other, frantically trying to elucidate which of them had called which other of them a slag. Of course, a great number of other people on Twitter also saw this fight and found it grimly hilarious, piling in and making it even worse.

A month or two later I heard from someone I vaguely knew, a media studies teacher, who said that he had given his students an entire lecture based around SlagGate, as the whole debacle was now referred to by many. Oh, I said. Wow, I said. What was the title of the lecture, I ventured … had it been one about charity fundraising, er, or er, how women talk to each other online, or em, the benefits of getting your own name Twitter handle before anyone else could take it?

'No,' he replied. 'It was called How Not To Use The Internet.'

28

I did bring him home but I didn't mean to rub the baby sick onto him

It began well enough. I met him at Eva's birthday party, which was in a crowded basement bar, and somehow we started kissing on the dancefloor like that was a thing that people still did. I was wearing a brightly coloured blouse that I had bought in a vintage clothes shop at some previous time when life had felt full of possibilities, and long before the kissing began he said that the blouse looked like curtains, which meant he was negging me, which is a cheap psychological trick in which you flirt by saying negative things about someone you desire to make their ego seek your approval, which in turn leads them to make more effort to impress you. You know, like how a vaccination gives the body a taste of the disease to stimulate the immune system into generating its own cure. The negged person, when they finally receive a compliment, will experience it as doubly rewarding, which will trick their reward-zone endorphins into wild excitement until they end up accidentally having sex with you. That's the plan, anyway – the compliment that the negative person gives doesn't even have to be that nice, just something that a normal person would have said in the first place, except this is London, so don't hold your breath.

As a sophisticated metropolitan individual, I instantly recognised that this guy was negging me, but as a person also gripped by the overriding horror of trying to look sexually attractive while dancing while not drunk enough yet, I also began to think that perhaps my blouse really did look like curtains. By the time he finally said something incredibly generous like, 'Well, I'm getting another drink, do you want one then?' I was overcome by the yearning to feel the warmth of his lips on mine.

So we got our drinks and then there was the kissing, and then more talking, and then somehow the sway of the party separated us, as parties do, throwing you into conversation with someone else, only to get moved onto someone else again, and constantly being interrupted when you were three-quarters of the way towards your punch-line, only to find yourself now three conversations past your prey. Parties are an exercise in a stop-motion choreography that brings you together and moves you apart, together and apart, but inside which you are all ultimately stuck, and you know you're all going to get vomited out onto the same street eventually. And sometimes you only go through the whole rigmarole of the first bit to find out what happens on the street, at the kicking-out part.

Sometimes I think that's my favourite moment – the bit where the fresh, cold air outside hits you, and the sun is going to rise in a few hours, and how can you keep the party motion going inside you, who will go with you, what now?

So Eva's party was coming to a close and Patrick was thrown back to me by the motion of the crowd, the surge of humans tossed about like Jonah inside the whale. But he had to leave – his friends were dragging him away – and so I said he should take my phone number and he tried to play it cool and said don't tell me what to do, and so I said fine, and then he said all right can I have your number, and I said no. And then I think there was maybe one more kiss, because we were really trying to annoy each other now.

So I went home, alone, and I paid the babysitter and sent her home, and then I checked on the baby and kissed her goodnight again, in her sleep, where she looked like a little piece of heaven broken from the sky and turned into human flesh, and then I went into my room, took all my clothes off and did what any red-blooded woman would do at this juncture. I got into bed, naked, and with both my hands, I took hold of my iPhone, went into my Twitter profile and edited my bio to delete any mention of the baby. Then I cropped her out of my profile photo and re-uploaded the zoomed-in, slightly wonkier version of the same photo with only me in it. And then I deleted all my recent tweets that had mentioned having a baby, and I took the photo of my daughter off my blog, locked my Instagram account, and changed all descriptions of me that I could find around the entire internet that might have either contained the word 'mother' or 'single mum' or 'pregnant' in them, which took some time, because my data footprint is large enough to frighten a yeti. Deleting my new life was strangely satisfying, although taking down the pregnancy photos did make me feel rather wistfully sad, because when else was he going to see my boobs looking so massive?

And then I fell asleep, delighted in the knowledge that Patrick probably hadn't had a chance to google me yet, but that when he did, I would appear in digital perfection as the old me, the one who was fun and free and floating and didn't have a child. Not that I could hide this fact from him for ever – and it wasn't that I was *ashamed*, in fact, I *longed* to tell him all about my beautiful little girl, and would definitely do so just as soon as we'd got through our wedding.

The next day Eva texted me and said Patrick had asked her for my email address, because I had refused him my phone number after I had offered it. *Perfection*, I thought – the revenge negging had worked and the humiliation of desire was now *his*, oh happy day, we would be married in a small but architecturally memorable country church. I texted her back giving my permission to pass it on, and also confessing to the Highland Clearances that I had performed on the internet in anticipation.

And Eva replied, Sophie we'd told him about the baby before you even fell into the fireplace with him when you were kissing him, it's a thing that people know about you.

Oh, I said.

So Patrick and I began an email exchange, in which he linked to a website for a company that sold discount curtains which he thought I might dislike, and also asked me if I would like to go for a drink with him. I suggested a pub near my house, which he was familiar with, describing it by return email as 'wanky' and 'a bit full of twats', so then I insisted upon it. Especially since it had big leather Chesterfield sofas and Czech beers and in my mind this was indicative of the sophistication that the new me deserved, because I had changed. I was always changing, but this particular change apparently involved leather sofas. Some friends called Nadia and Becca were staying in my house at this point, because their new flat nearby had failed to be ready to rent on the agreed date, and so they had agreed to babysit.

Patrick and I met in the pub and ordered our pints of minimalist Czech beer that came in angular, non-traditional pint glasses. I wanted to order this particular beverage because I felt it made me look subtly sophisticated and yet simultaneously appealingly laddish and up for a good time. Patrick wanted to drink it because it was a drink. And so we got stuck into the chats that you have when you're getting to know someone.

It's always the same format: they tell you their funny stories, something that just happened during their day at work or on their journey to meet you, and then something comically vulnerable that inevitably links back to their childhood, and then something that makes you wonder how much longer you have to talk until you can find a place to get off with them that is hopefully even darker than the pub. Patrick told me about the fact he had grown up not all that far from here, and how he and his brother had been so awful that their mum hired an au pair who came from another country to live with them, but she resigned before her first day was over.

And so then I told him my funny stories, like the fact that I had had this baby with a guy who didn't love me, who had actually got together with someone else when I was pregnant, could you believe it, I mean, not that it was like we were really together anyway so I suppose it wasn't like he had left me for her *exactly*, in fact, the last time we had sex was the night I got pregnant, and that wasn't meant to happen because the doctors had just told me I was infertile, which was why I hadn't used a condom, the only time I hadn't used a condom for fuck's sake, and how I was now raising this baby on my own because after demanding a DNA test we had had this awful fall-out and now he'd stopped visiting us and he hadn't spoken to me in a year and it was just this perpetual state of not knowing if my child would ever meet her father again and I hadn't really slept properly in a long time because the breastfeeding had been really difficult and now she was on solid foods, but even still who needs sleep when you're working on your writing until two o'clock in the morning most nights to keep your family afloat, and yes, the absent father is still paying his monthly maintenance payments, which do help, and yes, my mother is very involved and has helped so much, but oh, there's an emotional price to pay for becoming dependent on your parents in your thirties.

'This,' said Patrick, 'is … so … *sad*.' It wasn't just his words he was spacing apart – we had begun the night sitting right beside each other on the sofa, but now his body had slunk far along it. I looked at him, 400 miles along our seating arrangement, and realised that my mouth had fallen open and my life had slipped out. Once again, I had done that classic thing of mistaking a first date with a potential boyfriend with a first treatment session with a registered psychiatrist, which is an easy mistake to make on a Chesterfield.

And I know it's not just me who does this, because of the alarming number of people (all right, women) who have that quote that Marilyn Monroe probably didn't even say on their online dating profile: 'If you can't handle me at my worst, you sure don't deserve me at my best.' A quote now as ubiquitous as the office signs of my childhood that read, 'You don't have to be mad to work here but it helps!' And even if Marilyn did say that, that people should be able to handle you at your worst, she is unlikely to have meant that they should be able to handle you at your worst at the very moment while they're taking their coat off and asking if you'd like a drink.

What you have to do is trust in the fact that your worst is something that will come up anyway, during the passage of time, ideally when love has already had a chance to find its footing. Your worst has enough gravity of its own to make itself felt, you don't have to give it a seat at the table and buy it a Staropramen and get it to thank everyone for coming to its TED Talk. Also Marilyn Monroe died alone of a barbiturate overdose at thirty-six. I'm just saying.

Still, this is just what happens if you've been single for a while and your romantic mind has started to wander. Because when a person has been single for some time, their hope does not dwindle. Quite the opposite: it explodes. They start to think they're being pursued by the biggest love imaginable. They think love is coming for them down the street like the Grim Reaper, like an unstoppable madman with an axe. It's there. They can feel it. They wonder what it is going to taste like, but they think they know. They look into the stars and they see it. They miss their flight and suddenly it's a sign that the biggest love imaginable will be in the airport at the end of the later flight, waiting to be bumped into at baggage reclaim.

Being single is like being left in charge of a library book that hasn't had a date stamped in it. You don't know when the call is going to come, just that it will come, because it has to come, this ultimate of ultimates. The single person wants to shave her legs to make sure she's ready. And then she wants *not* to shave her legs, to tempt fate into letting love arrive when she's looking the other way, all hairy and unprepared. The attached person smiles at this single person and laughs, saying, 'Bless you, you're trying too hard, why, love will come when you least expect it.' The single person is irritated and sits there with a furrowed brow, *furiously* least expecting it and least expecting it. The single person reads all this guff about how nobody will love her until she loves herself, and so she becomes ever more determined to love herself. She loves herself with the force of a small child trying to prise the lid off a jar of peanut butter.

The single person imagines that love will make him into a better man, and so he tempts fate by becoming a worse man. The single person wonders about his other half, and so he throws himself down rabbit holes, to drink from the bottle marked 'Drink Me', and eat the cake marked 'Eat Me', and try to reach the feeling where he has become both halves himself. The single person is powered by nervous energy, convinced that he is on the hook, and that the greatest love imaginable will get him off it. Sometimes, he wonders if a relationship will accelerate his mass to a stated velocity, like they taught him in physics lessons, in those words that have been rumbling around his head for years, with the stated velocity now being ALL OF THE MUSIC, ALL OF THE FUCKING TIME. But this might just be the 'Eat Me' and the 'Drink Me' talking, and it might be nonsense, but it will make sense when she finds him.

Really, all you people who are actually in love should be jealous of single people. We're having the biggest love affair imaginable! Much bigger than yours. We don't even hear you when you complain that living together isn't that great because it's only been two years and already the sex has dropped off and it's just become this sort of arrangement where your spouse isn't so much your soul-mate as just that person who passes you in the kitchen, asking why you haven't given the cat its eye drops. A single person can't even hear you when you say this. Because the longer a person is single, the more ultimate their big love becomes, the time spent alone being directly proportional to the increase in its size. Until the single person's love grows so large that it threatens to invade small countries, print its own stamps and compose a national anthem. Single people dream of a love so big that a wrestler can't lift it, so loud that Rammstein can't deafen it, a love so morbidly obese that it has to be winched out through the roof, pursued by a TV documentary crew as it makes its way to the stomach-stapling operation in a jumbulance.

Anyway. It was at this point that Patrick realised there was a noise coming from his phone. Not a ringing or a beeping noise, but a strange sort of mumbling. He looked at it and realised that at some point, probably when trying to save his entire body from collapsing under the weight of my confessional, his elbow had leaned onto it, and it had rung somebody. To be specific, it had rung his ex-girlfriend, who was now on the line, and who had possibly been listening to our conversation for some time. God she must have been jealous – how could she ever hope to win him back, now that she knew he was dating in the league of hot sexy chat about emergency Caesarean sections and direct debit child-maintenance payment plans?

I now wanted to look at my own phone, for company or perhaps to stove my own head in with, hard to be sure which exactly. At which point I discovered that, in my desire to speak at length about the pressures of looking after my daughter, I had missed four calls and three texts from the people who were looking after my daughter. This could only mean one thing: the baby was dead. I rang them back while standing up and grabbing my bag. The baby wasn't dead, I soon discovered, but she had gone pale and vomited several times, and they said they had run out of blankets that she hadn't puked on and why wasn't I answering my phone and coming home immediately?

Sometimes your heart really does skip a beat.

I screamed at Patrick what was happening and said we had to run to my house – he had no choice but to come with me – and so we ran. I didn't even stop to put my drink down, which meant that when we got there, out of breath and terrified, I charged into my house to clutch my sick baby while still holding an aspirational pint of lifestyle lager in my hand. With hindsight, the optics on that weren't great.

Fortunately, my friends had done an absolutely excellent job of looking after the baby, as well as googling all her symptoms and coming to a quite reasoned diagnosis of the norovirus, which they said we were probably all about to come down with, given the close proximity in which we were all living. The baby was now safely restored to her cot, fast asleep, breathing fine, monitor on, living her best norovirus life. And look, I'm not going to pretend that, after sitting with her for some time, I should then have left my child's side for a single moment ever again, but life is a trip and my heart was beating so loud I actually thought it would wake her. I tiptoed downstairs where Patrick was sitting politely at the kitchen table, genuinely concerned. He was actually a really nice person. I could see that now. Shit.

And I was only an occasional smoker but my nerves started rummaging through the kitchen drawer for one of my old, stale, emergency cigarettes, and I told Patrick we were going to sit in the backyard for a minute. He made it clear that he was going to do nothing of the kind because a) he hated smoking, and b) it was the middle of winter and absolutely fucking freezing outside. Naturally, I dragged him out to the frosty picnic table regardless, where I lit up and began to rant some more, as if I could somehow outweigh the effects of the earlier rant by ranting over the top of it with another one. Then I drank the second half of my pint. Patrick started to shiver. He looked cold. Oh he really looked cold. But then, wait, how handy – weirdly, as if by magic, there were some blankets on the patio, so I wrapped him up in them at the picnic table and he shivered a bit less after that, though he did say he should probably be getting home.

He prepared to depart and I did the only sensible thing I could think of: I launched myself in to kiss him. He sort of went along with it, I think perhaps because it helped him propel our bodies nearer to the front door so he could leave. Or perhaps because he worked with vulnerable people for his day job and saw this as some form of care in the community – hard to be certain. But there was a kiss, and then he was gone. The door closed behind him and I took a deep breath for the first time in weeks. Maybe months. Maybe years.

And the thought struck me that – oh God it was obvious. He'd have stuck around if only I hadn't smoked! I went outside to clear up the ashtray, wondered again what those blankets had actually been doing, so helpfully left there on a cold evening in winter, and then, only then, realised that they were the ones covered in highly contagious vomit that my babysitting friends had felt weren't safe to be kept inside the house. The stains were quite apparent now – and the lumps. Of sick. Oh, I thought. Ah. Still, it was a relief, really, to know that I hadn't given him the norovirus by kissing him with my fag breath as he tried to escape my house – he would have already contracted the illness when I wrapped him in the vomitous blankets.

If there is anything truly wrong with the state of my mind, it is the tendency to believe, deep down, not that everything is terrible, but that everything is, actually, wonderful – which will become apparent when you learn that I still went to bed ranking this date in the section of my mind marked *promising*. And that I texted Patrick the next morning, while the baby sat playing with Duplo in front of me and I made funny faces at her and she only cried a little bit, to say what a night it had been! And that he texted me straight back eighteen hours later to say yes, really *quite* a memorable evening for everyone concerned.

29

East London baby rave

The anxiety set in when I realised that the German family on my bus, dressed entirely in camouflage, leopard skin and fake fur, were going to the same place I was. A baby rave, in a nightclub, from three till six on a Sunday afternoon. Come and listen to banging techno with the kids, said my friends, it'll be a laugh! Then I got there and the queue was already around the block, one hundred parents with their offspring, their deely boppers and their tortured hope. It looked quite a lot like the Boden catalogue, if all the children's faces had been painted over by Hieronymous Bosch. My one-year-old was with me in her pushchair, chewing on her own hand. Joining the queue, I found myself asking God – much like when I peed on a stick two years ago, actually – if this was really happening to me.

Inside, things were crowded and banging. Some seven-year-olds were deep in chat on the stairs, engaged in some nefarious tangerine dealing, with an older man clearly trying to push pistachios. Toddlers ran past me screaming, visibly off their chops on ketamine, or sweets. The main room was pumping out K-Klass, which simultaneously made me so excited and terrified that we had to run away into the chill-out room, where a jovial old Father Christmas lookalike was playing a bunch of rare groove and soul. My friends from the ante-natal class, some of whom, like Hannah and Gemma, had turned out to be old ravers too, were in there with all of their confused babies. Somebody passed me a beer, and I put my child down to dance so she got to work pulling out all the electrical wires from the back of the decks, and then burning her finger on a very hot set of fairy lights. It was at this point I realised I had done entirely the right thing by bringing her here.

Raves were the making of me. Illegal ones in fields somewhere near a roundabout off the A64, or semi-illegal ones in dusty warehouses with structural issues. Legal parties in nightclubs full of attitude. The quite fancy club in Leeds where there was a power cut, and when the lights came back on a couple were having penetrative sex on the nicely carpeted stairs. The one where I went to Manchester to meet my friend and then ended up spending two days with a new friend in Otley (he wore dungarees and was kind). The gay night in Leeds that the straight lads loved so much the transvestite bouncers started making them kiss each other before they could go in. The outdoors one that we were approaching when the police stopped us, and my friend Phil – who was driving and skinning up at that point – talked boring stoner shit at them for such a long time that they just couldn't *bear* it any longer and waved us through.

But what I really learned from raving was how to lose yourself dancing in a crowd of strangers, who you can love even without talking to them. In fact, it's better if you don't stop dancing to talk to them, as more than two minutes of conversation often reveals that they are a pathological racist, the sort of person who reuses teabags and has constructed a complicated faith system about their local car wash. A person who, when you pass them the office stapler, says 'Monkey magic!' by way of thanks, and then cracks their knuckles and says 'Bad habit!' and 'Mental, eh!' A person who would be about as popular in your real life as that Microsoft Office paperclip, or the Comic Sans typeface, if it had been gifted a driving licence and legs.

At the dance, though, you love these people and you are one of them. Because if you've never been hugged by a stranger in a darkness only lit by lasers with pure happiness swelling up inside you, you haven't lived! Occasionally, it's good to liberate yourself from the exhaustion of holding all your love in every day – man, it's so tiring being English, and keeping all of this passion in here. If it wasn't taboo I'd touch people on the bus. I'd run my hands through children's hair. I'd wrap my fingers around the driver's face and say, 'How long do you think it will take to get to the ends of the Earth together?' I'd have sex with all of my friends if there weren't repercussions, and I know all about the repercussions, as there was a good chunk of 2003 when I was quite committed to field research in this area.

(Back at the baby rave, they're playing a song like 'Je t'aime' – it's not that, but it's got a breathy orgasm bit where a female voice groans with pleasure, and a seven-year-old girl has grabbed the microphone and is groaning along with it, and nobody has noticed. I don't know who I am any more.)

But most of all, I want my daughter to know the joy of being squashed by the otherpeopleness of other people, particularly the ones who you might scroll right past on a dating website or turn down at a job interview, because in the end you're just one of life's 8,000 teeth. I'm not raising her to think she's the one in a million that can make a difference – that way madness lies. All this propaganda going out to kids today that they matter! I want her to know that she doesn't matter at all and that none of this is real. I want her to revel in the freedom of being born an unplanned human being. Nobody painted a nursery for her, nobody set aside a college fund or organised the person they wanted her to become. All this stuff about working hard so you can be the best and stand out from the rest – I think it might be capitalism's cleverest trick of all. Teaching you to think that this is how you count.

And so I wish her the joy of being anyone, for a few hours, lost in the darkness, answerable only to the molecules. If anything, I want her to know that she is nobody, and nothing. I want her to feel like air.

30

I attend an office party and meet an elegant penis

It is 11 p.m. and a man and I are standing in the dark and cold in a garden square in East London, a couple of minutes' walk from a media party which is still going on. I've been really getting my writing going again, and getting noticed for it after starting a weekly column on the *Vice* website. *Vice* is an online and print magazine which delights and appals people in equal measure, with its hipsters and tits and snide young things, untrained reporters who seem to think nothing of conducting interviews with strangers in the street while on drugs, or tunnelling into Syria to get a quote from a group of rebel fighters in person. It is 2013 and the brand is riding high in the media, with more established companies paying close and nervous attention, because *Vice* holds sway with millennials who aren't engaging with telly and newspapers otherwise. Even the Murdochs are sniffing around. Writing this column means I've been getting invited to the sort of parties where you can start arguments with hipsters again, and Diane has moved in with us for a bit, which means I can go to them. She prefers to stay in and start arguments with the telly.

Come with me, Sophie, this guy says, panting like a dog with sweaty parts and good intentions, or intentions that at least seem good to a dog. He grabs my hand. He's taken an E, though I can't tell what he plans to do with his high, or which side of it he is currently on. I'm not sure he knows either. He says he needs to walk, so we duck out into the cold. Now we've reached the square, which contains a kids' playground that I actually came to last week with some of the mums from my antenatal group, whom I have fondly come to think of as the Hallouminati, since that's what their children seem to live on. Not in a Turkish way; more in a lifestyle sandwich kind of vibe. My own child's food preferences, meanwhile, are depressingly Brexit, based almost exclusively around wheat and potato starch. None of that foreign muck for her.

The shabby old roundabout had been particularly popular with our toddlers, with one of them enjoying it so much that he made a good start on licking it before his mother removed him. This had happened only shortly after my own toddler had leant out of her buggy while I was looking at my phone, and licked a bus stop on the Cambridge Heath Road. The thing about toddlers is that they get the most sensation from their mouth – more than through their fingers – which is why they want to put everything inside it. Now I was back in the same square in the darkness, though I wasn't sure why – perhaps my colleague wanted to heft his buttocks into the tiny seats and spin around on the roundabout before licking it too. Perhaps this was all that any grown adult longed to do with themself. Get that toddler feeling back into their tongue.

'You see all this,' my friend continued, his other hand roaming upwards, and I dearly hoped that he was gesturing at the big Georgian houses that surrounded the square, with their sagging windows and black railings, because I was constantly looking them up on property websites and planning how I would use the space when I moved in, and wondering whether I could get planning permission to knock through the kitchen and dining room when they were Grade 2 listed or if I'd just have to keep the rooms aspirationally dark and poky à la *World of Interiors*.

'What we have created is – a space,' he said. Or was he talking about the internet? The dark and poky online universe we worked inside? Now I'm not saying I was sober – I had obviously had a few drinks to take the edge off the pain of existence and the doom of humanity rumbling through my brain as per, but my chat was still tight. This guy, though, was talking bobbins like he meant it. 'We've created a space where, you, me, the others—' he stopped to name a few people who we socialised with and worked with, because they were all the same people, because that was how this scene worked. And they were all at the party. 'We've all taken something really *powerful* … and imbued it with power. But like, really different, different power. Like a charged, box, of, self-same, powered self.'

This is the thing about drugs – if you have never taken them, you might have been led to believe that they take you to an unreal state, where things suddenly feel magical and crazy and wild. In fact, they do the exact opposite, and take you to a state where everything suddenly feels absolutely real and normal, in a way that things never do in so-called real life. Nobody in their working day believes that the work they're conducting is *'a charged box of power'*. When I'm sober, I'm not convinced that anything I do really counts at all – I barely even believe that things will continue to exist if I stop looking at them. Does a tree make a sound when it falls in the forest if there's nobody there to hear it, people used to ask smugly when I was at university, and I'd be thinking to myself *what forest? There is no forest*, which possibly explains why I dropped out and went to work in a shoe shop for light relief.

But I digress.

'Kiss me,' he said.

'No,' I said.

'*Kiss* me,' he said, surprised that it hadn't worked the first time and repeating the words as if checking them for holes.

'Don't be *silly*,' I replied in a tone that could almost be described as maternal, while wondering if it was too late to redirect his tongue towards that slag of a roundabout.

Then he reached for me, so I knocked him off his balance, which was at least easy, because he had, at this moment, all the physical control of a Trebor softmint. I had not taken any ecstasy and so I knew something that my co-worker didn't, which was that he didn't fancy me, not really. This wasn't some long-held desire coming out. He didn't want power over me either. No, he was merely

209

feeling that synthetic rush of feelings where you want everything in the world to be possible all at once.

But this was getting embarrassing. So I decided to take control and march him back to the party. It worked for about twenty yards before he realised what was happening, and yanked us to an abrupt stop to make his final protest.

'You really should do this,' he said, gesturing at his ravishing human form, all that I was missing. 'Because …'

And then he added these five magic little words, which I shall never forget as long as I live:

'… I have a majestic penis.'

Still, the column was a success, for the year that it ran. One day I went to get a bikini wax, not something I had done before, even in the Hollywood years. I was a hairy seventies bush sort of woman, but everything was new now – maybe I should try something different, who bloody knows, give it a whirl. So I went to a beauty salon in Shoreditch and just as this young woman was taking off the paper knickers they make you put on before they apply hot wax to the outside of your genitals, she cried out 'Oh, *I* know who you are!' How she had worked this out from the sight of my vagina, I don't really wish to imagine. The beautician then told me all about how she didn't really like the other stuff on *Vice* but she loved my column and read it every week. I'm not sure if this made it harder or easier for me to ask the question pursed on my lips, which was, could she please leave enough of my pubes intact to cover the scar from my Caesarean.

Oh, East London. You're a vibe, all right.

31

In which I bore on about insufferable bores

Y ou weren't really allowed to compliment your children when I grew up. I remember once asking my mother if I was pretty. She wasn't really listening so she said yes. Then she looked up from the *Radio Times* and actually contemplated my face. 'Well,' she began again.

Yet somehow, between my childhood and my daughter's childhood, the parents of Britain have become insufferable bores, constantly praising their children and telling everyone else how wonderful they are too. Bigging up their own slavish devotion to parenting methods, which are, naturally, superior to yours. Sometimes it is done as humblebragging, which is a boast dressed up as self-deprecation, something which seems particularly popular among new parents.

'Can you believe my baby has never tasted sugar! I'm such a geek, such a library mum,' they will say, a statement that is designed to make you feel subtly inferior as

211

it will unfailingly be announced at the table where your own child is tucking into a Kit Kat that fell out of your handbag, guided by your hand. (It will also be said by the sort of person who buys a £125 printed navy sweatshirt that says G E E K on it.)

These humblebraggers will slyly inspect your every parenting move, delivering the strangest of backhanded compliments, such as, 'Oh, your child is so clever, isn't she, we had to start potty-training ours well before he was two because we knew how long it would take with him, such a job on our hands! It must be because yours is SO intelligent that you're fine with her still being crappy in a nappy at twenty-six months!'

The secret joy of being a single parent is that you are simply never going to have the time for all this perfectionism as you're already in a massive compromise – your shtick is never going to be watertight. But the thing is, you will see through other people's perfection too, and soon learn to decode their performances. To realise that when somebody says, 'We don't have plastic toys in our house', what they actually mean is, 'We feel weird about the decade we spent snorting gak every Friday night and must purge it from our memories in the desperate craving of forgiveness and purity.' Similarly, 'We will never use disposable nappies' directly translates as 'We have never actually changed a nappy before', just as 'We're practising attachment parenting' means, 'We have decided never to have sex in this marriage again.' And then there's the classic, 'My wife has never left our baby to cry for more than a second because we didn't want to traumatise him,' which means 'Subtly anti-feminist propaganda has convinced me that a woman's sanity isn't the point.'

I have watched my generation of parents turn into Lady Macbeth, out damn spot out, not letting their child have candy floss at the fair, even though said child was conceived on a three-day bender, which began at a family wedding and ended in a ditch five miles from the nearest Wetherspoons. My generation of parents are the same people who experienced the mass marketing of coolness in the early 2000s, when cool went from something belonging to the occasional brilliant freak like David Bowie to being widely available at Urban Outfitters instead. And so we have become the Urban Outfitter hipster parents, dressing our children in blue-and-white Breton stripes and feeding them halloumi and teaching them to call their penises penises and their vaginas vaginas, no, wait, it's vulva now. These yummy mummies and rad dads all form part of secret Hallouminati groups whose membership codes are shrouded in ancient rituals involving dried mango, colour-coded Tupperware and half-term holidays at child-friendly festivals in Dorset. Their children have all been given so many books about Amazing Women in History that any one of them will now eye up a new picture book very warily, muttering that this one better not be about Frida Kahlo again.

We crave this purity, this neat jaunty perfectness, because our parents or their parents came from families who knew bombs and war, something that was never fully explained to us, it just lurked, hanging about in their buried trauma, in the pain they weren't really allowed to feel and thus we weren't really allowed to feel either. But we knew we were missing something, and so now we hold our own children closer, and present our babies as fashion statements: look how I have matched my clothes to my child's clothes in this heavily filtered photo on the internet, and look how, even though I embrace the hashtags #mentalhealth and #anxiety and #wellness, you will never see in the picture what happens to my mind when my beautiful matching baby cries, and cries, and cries.

32

The Artist

I met the Artist on Tinder while on a trip back to LA to see my old haunts. I had only downloaded it, after a year or so without looking at dating apps, because my friend Lily wanted me to see how awful the Tinder men in LA now were. So we scrolled through it laughing at their awfulness, topless and rippled, hunting big game, or on a mountainside head to toe in full snowboarding gear, so no part of their body could be seen apart from their wealth. And then I found the Artist, who had scruffy hair and an untucked shirt and was playing table tennis in someone's backyard. He had an easy smile that did not suggest an addiction to prescription drugs or a mother who had never loved him or a father who had told him he would never amount to anything if he didn't get the biggest muscles in his prep school. The profile said he liked to paint and he liked to kiss and he liked to be in Echo Park. I liked all of these things too, and I liked him liking them.

I followed a link he had posted and discovered a website full of beautiful paintings, mergings of rich, dark colours

– they really had something strange and special about them. I felt a rush of excitement when we matched – this meant he had liked my profile too. But what was I doing? This was just a trip and I hadn't expected to meet someone this way. I had to break it to him, as soon as we started to chat, that I was only in LA for a couple more weeks and that I lived back in London now. 'I guess you're not The One then,' he replied, which made me laugh, especially when he continued that he would still like to meet me. Three days later we met up in a dark bar called The Short Stop at 8 p.m. and when he walked in I looked at the skin on his face and felt a word come from it: benevolence. I've never felt a word come from anyone's skin before, but all I can tell you is that on that night, in that place, with only one sip of drink in me, that is exactly what happened. His face and my face looked at one another and it was as easy as water. Oh, I thought – it's *you*.

The night progressed. We did the chat about our families, discovered that he studied philosophy at university, which my father teaches, and that I did Latin American Studies, which his father *is*, and this made such a perfect shape in my head that I could see nothing but the joining of a circle. A mirrored circle made of us. We both spoke warmly of our backgrounds. Benevolence. I took all of this as an absolute sign of our perfection in mirrored form. I take everything as a sign. When a woman's sex organs want to find a sign that the universe is willing them to be sexually linked to another person's organs, a woman's sex organs will find them.

We were on Sunset Boulevard, but not the famous Hollywood part of it. Further down the most easterly stretch of it, in Echo Park, an area once famous for moustachioed Mexican gangs but now a little quieter on the rivalry front, a lot of their former haunts having been colonised by beardy hipsters. With gentrification, facial hair had slipped down the face. These bearded hipsters were all unique in wanting to do the exact same things as each other. They wanted to use VHS tapes instead of DVDs, cassettes instead of USB music systems in their car, drink whisky sours instead of Jagermeister bombs, install photobooths in their bars for vintage selfies. Record players, love letters, plaits in their hair. Perhaps they held some oblique desire to rid the world of themselves, to uninvent themselves, to go back to the time just before they were conceived. Perhaps to rid the world of their own parents having sex. Back to a time before Wi-Fi ran through our veins like blood. They all used iPhones though, obviously – these were hipsters who liked to digitally document their fetishisation of a pre-digital world.

But the Artist was a gentle mixture of all of these things. He was a hipster, perhaps, but his parents, grandparents, had come to El Norte, to this country, from Mexico, in search of better things. His moustache was both ironic and genuine. His facial hair spoke of many things at once. But he was short so nobody noticed anyway. And he actually came from the suburbs of Sacramento, and barely spoke twenty words of Spanish, unlike me, who was fairly fluent, having done half a degree in it. But this couldn't stop me exoticising him.

We have a couple of drinks in that bar until it closes. He says he knows somewhere else to go that is open later, and this turns me on. My friend is back at the place where my daughter and I are staying, babysitting, and she has said to stay out as late as I want, no holds barred, enjoy yourself. So I say okay. Not that I have told him about the babysitter, or about the baby. I just say okay.

He orders an Uber, and I don't really notice where it's taking us because I have eyes only for the Artist, but when we get out of the car in some awful deserted kind of underpass beside the freeway, it drives away and I look around and say, there is no bar here, there's nothing here. I wonder if this is where I will meet my death.

Yes there is, he says, and he opens a door in a wall that doesn't have any doors in it. And through this magic door is an old-school Los Angeles speakeasy, a secret afterhours piano bar full of people, heaving with life, where somebody's playing jazz piano down one end of the room, and he gets us a couple of cocktails from the bar and the place is so rammed, tiny but rammed, that the only seats left are right down opposite the piano. We keep drinking and talking and then I say I have to tell him something. I tell him I have a kid. He looks startled. I tell him that the reason I haven't mentioned her yet is because she is so wonderful that if I start talking about her I will never stop, and that that will get boring for him. (I have learned now, how to do this.)

He says, and her dad? And I say, no, we're not together at all, we split up at the start. I still dread telling this part of the story, which to me is ugly and weird because – how the hell did this happen, how did I end up with a child who doesn't know her father, how is this my life, where is my paddock, my farmhouse in Wales, my Aga, my love? He looks relieved. And I realise that he's relieved there's no angry ex-boyfriend lurking in my life to make trouble for anyone.

When I ask him later, some days later, how our first kiss happened, it is because I genuinely long to know. I remember the piano bar, I remember the important conversation; our confessions beside a dance floor. I remember, also, the kissing. But what I don't remember is how it began. How did we go from not kissing to kissing? My mind is blank only for that bit of the night. 'You basically,' he says, when asked, 'sort of fell on me and attacked me.' He is perfectly happy about this.

And because the only seats available are in front of the piano, which everyone is focused on, the focal point of the room, everyone is now looking at us. At some point it is decided we need a room. We go back to his place, a strange basement in Echo Park. You go inside and it's down what feels like a fire escape metal staircase, only it's indoors, not out, and it takes you down into a windowless basement, the sort of which I have never seen in this city of light. It's a studio space with a kitchen in one corner but he lives in it too. It's dark. It's odd. We fall into bed and our attempts at warm and frenzied longing are exciting but soon they are hampered by our cocktailed brains. We fall asleep. I awake a few hours later, realising I absolutely have to get home before my kid wakes up. I get myself together, rummage around and pull my missing underwear back on, creep up the staircase. I leave him a note on the kitchen table. I can't remember what it says, something nice.

I get out onto the street, it's still dark, 5 a.m., and I want to order an Uber and the only way I find out where I am is by looking at the GPS on my phone when I order an Uber. It's the walk of shame, only in a car. The driver asks me, as we drive our way through the dark into the steeper streets of Echo Park, if I'm going to work now. What *is* he suggesting, I wonder.

So what I remember is leaving his place, going back to mine, and the weeks that followed, of us falling further in love, me and my daughter going back to London and him booking flights to follow shortly afterwards. More love.

It was different when he was in London. I noticed, back in my sunless, harder city, that he didn't know what he was doing all the time, didn't know how to find places, had never used public transport, being a suburban American kid who'd learned to drive down straight grid-system roads aged sixteen. I felt like my mother as the desire to snap and sneer rose up in me. Why didn't he know these things that he had no way of knowing until he knew them? I realised I was a harder person in London than in LA. I started to realise that the reason I felt more loved in LA than in London might have been because a certain spell fell over me there, relaxing me. Here, in my own country, I wanted him to be an all-invincible man who could do everything and master everything and be in control of everything. And yet I also wanted a feminine man who, when seeing I was reading Chris Kraus's *I Love Dick*, a really investigative feminist novel about something much more nuanced and complicated than loving dick, said that he had liked her earlier book so much that he had emailed her and they'd struck up an ongoing correspondence of sorts. He did do this. It was intriguing.

And his paintings were really beautiful. His jokes about art made me laugh. He made me come a hundred times in a hundred places. And now I wanted him to be twice his size with a full knowledge of how London worked. I was being too hard on him, I said to myself.

One night, in bed in London, he says, maybe we could do role play. And I think, oh boy. This is a thing I have read about in magazines but never done. Do people actually do this? Then he says, we could be a doctor and a patient! And I think – I am lying, I have totally done this. In fact, I did this for what felt like a full twelve hours yesterday. Should I tell him that it was on this same bed that my daughter and I set up the mock hospital with a purple doctor's kit, four teddy bears and two dolls all waiting to be seen, and where I had to stretch my daughter's leg out into the X-ray machine (a ripped open cardboard box that had delivered an electric hand blender to our house) to see how badly it was broken, and that it turns out that there is a limit to how many municipal health centres I can set up in a forty-eight hour period?

I want to be open to this idea. I don't want to be old. I don't want to be boring. I don't want him to be in bed with somebody's mum, which is an ontological conundrum because he is in bed with somebody's mum, and my dad, the philosophy lecturer, is quite big on ontological conundrums, so maybe I should ring him up and say hey, how is it possible that I can take a break from the rest of my life to be a young sexy adventurer in bed with a new man and open to all the possibilities while also being someone's mum? Is that a thing? Also, can I just take my head off and put on a different head? I do not ring my father with any of these queries.

Then the child screams and I leap out of bed, leaving him in it. He got here at 10.30 at night when she was already asleep, and he will be out of this bed and on the sofa with a blanket and a pillow before she wakes. She doesn't know he sleeps in here. She cries for me, a wrong turn taken in dreaming, a duvet that has twisted into a dragon. A curtain flapping in the draught that has turned into a spectre. She cries out for a shot of me, her night milk, and then I go back to him, to be his night milk, and to get my night milk too. The night contains multitudes in which I have a starring role.

One time I'm sent on a work trip to LA for about forty-eight hours and it's perfect as I can leave my daughter with my parents and stay with him and we can have a tiny window of time together, just for us. Me and the Artist.

We get up together on the second morning. We both get dressed, he drinks some coffee, I make nervous noises because I have to interview an actress at the Chateau Marmont and this always makes me nervous even though I've done it many times. I tell him I'll be back at around 3 p.m. and he says he'll probably be there but he gives me a set of keys in case he's out. I come back around 3 p.m. as promised and I put one key into the door. I realise that it is not double-locked and that he must be in. Our remaining time together is so brief that I'm pleased. The interview has gone really well, and now we have one more night together.

So I let myself in and walk down the sort of indoor fire escape staircase that leads into his strange cavern of a living space. There is an enormous curtain that hides this staircase from the room, and it is only when you are halfway down that you can peek out from behind the curtain and see into the rest of the area, where the bed is. But you can instantly see the kitchen area and the table, which is where I left him, fully dressed, drinking coffee and working at his laptop. He is not at the table any more.

I walk further down the stairs and realise that something is playing quite loudly, is it the radio? A man's voice is talking. A man's voice that sounds strangely familiar, though it's nobody I know, and not the Artist.

More steps down and I can see that the Artist is lying on his bed, with his projector on a ledge behind him, screening a movie on the big white wall in front of him. Strangely, the Artist is no longer fully dressed, like I left him this morning. He is lying on his white sheets, white pillows, white covers, white bed, naked. He has one sheet artfully lain over half of his body. The rest of him, hairy, petite, perfectly formed, is exposed. Why is he watching a film while naked? Oh—

I glance, with some trepidation and a grinding feeling of inevitability in my belly, towards the wall, where this spectacle, if he himself wasn't enough of one, is writ large. He sometimes uses these big white walls as gallery space for events, but now it is a cinema, showing the movie several feet wide. I know that it is going to be porn and I don't know what I'm going to do. It has taken the focus from me and him and our precious time together, and shifted it somewhere well beyond that wall.

I'm not against porn. I sometimes enjoy porn. But I have to dig deep for the stuff I like, because nearly all the other stuff is horrible and grabby and shaven. Is he doing this because he forgot I was coming back or because he knew? Is he naked because he's … yeah.

This is all buzzing through my brain as I walk further down the stairs and he turns to look at me and says, in the most theatrical, slow turn of the head way, 'Ohh, *hi* babe,' like he's a gigolo I've just hired in a brothel. 'Hi!' I say, short and snappy, like the normal person I am so desperately trying to be right now. And then I have to do it. I have to reach the bottom of the stairs and turn my body right round so I can see the film itself, see exactly which wretched skinny sex slave with a shaven haven is having their face rammed into a big creaming cock.

That is not what I see.

What I see is a man in glasses and cords and a brown turtleneck sweater walking down a street in Holland and talking about painting. In about 1982. Everyone else is wearing clothes too. Awful clothes. Because what the film turns out to be is an Open University documentary about the life of Rembrandt, presented by an Englishman who has clearly never had sex in his life, or at least not with another person in the room, and who is walking the streets of Leiden, Rembrandt's hometown, talking about the great Dutch artist's life and times in seventeenth-century Holland. It is a show that was clearly originally shown on BBC2 in the early hours, for the committed students of my childhood. In fact, I may even have stumbled upon it myself, in those days when we only had three channels on the television, and sometimes Open University repeats were all there was to watch.

This old programme has been uploaded to YouTube, and my boyfriend has fed it through his projector and taken all his clothes off and got into bed and under the covers to watch it, for reasons that I do not wish to think about, not then, not now, not ever. I mean I've cracked some inappropriate ones out in my time but *never* over a man with a turtleneck sweater leading me through the streets of Leiden.

When the other mums at school ask if we are still moving to America I do not know quite what to tell them. 'Just sort of realised we were fundamentally different people,' I mutter, as we all stand outside Willow Class waiting for our little ones to run out of the door into our arms, and as I wait for the image of a man watching Rembrandt documentaries in the nude to disappear from my mind's eye for ever.

33

My daughter and I are a small republic

We are a small republic of two, my daughter and I. We sit at the breakfast table every morning, staring across at each other like Frost and Nixon. Every damn day. And every day she says, Mummy, look at my sad face. And I say, that's not very sad, look at *my* sad face, and I do a mournful expression the same as hers only I let my jaw hang down, wide open, and let one of my eyes tilt to the side, as if I am dying, and she giggles and says, no, Mummy look at *my* sad face, and she copies all of mine but adds an enormous sigh to it, a sigh that knocks her head practically off her neck, right onto its side, and so I say, look at *my* sad face and I do everything that she did but I also fall right off my chair on purpose and collapse onto the hard kitchen floor at some personal discomfort along with a crumb landing in my ear and I start to cry out, wailing loudly, rending my garments, 'I AM SO SAD, OH LORD, WHY HAST THOU FORSAKEN ME', and then my daughter is almost hysterical with rancid delight and joins me on the floor crying and crying out, 'OH LORD, WHY HAVE SHAKING', because that's what she thinks I've said, and then I bellow 'SACKCLOTH AND ASHES', and she shouts 'SACK OFF AND AFFING', and then the dog is shrieking, because we have got a new puppy, after I decided that I was pushing forty and there would be no more children, and the puppy is jumping all over us, demented by everyone being on the floor, barking into us, and there's a paw in my mouth and black fur in my daughter's ears and we're all screaming and fighting him off, and then we remember that it's 8.42 a.m. on a school day and I have to get her hair into two French plaits that I learned to do by watching the same YouTube instructional video eleven times.

We grab our coats and shoes and run along the street because we were too busy rending our garments and praying to God for forgiveness on our kitchen floor, but we get there before they close the gates at 9 a.m., we always make it just in the nick of time, and we hug each other goodbye, and she goes inside and goes up the stairs to her classroom, but she stops at the big landing window and waves down at me again, and we both bump a fist onto our hearts to show that we will carry each other in there all day, and then we blow a kiss and each of us do a big splat movement, a sort of fried-egg punch on our bodies, to show where the kiss that the other person blew has landed, and it is always some dreadful inappropriate landing place like an eye, an ear, a bra. Splat goes the imaginary kiss and we wipe it off ourselves. We mime, wordlessly, that we have each been wounded by the other's kiss.

And then she hurries on up the stairs to her classroom where she does all her schoolwork like the ambitious child she is, and I run out of the gates before the caretaker locks them, and I bury the grumbles about the unpaid tax bill and the unanswered emails in my belly, and I go on my way, pre-warmed, as if someone had put my second best bra on a radiator. I want all our days to begin with a love affair.

Some might think a romance between a parent and child is not healthy. What would they think if it came from a father who wanted his little girl to know that she was beautiful? Because I have had to provide both things, the romance and the rules. A single parent is both structure and playground, walls and soft landing, mother tropes and father tropes. Good cop and bad cop. I have degendered the situation and don't see myself as a mother, but as a parent, as the adult, as the introduction to what the world can be like. As neutral as passion, as pretty as heat. And what the world can be like, is wonderful.

You don't ready someone to travel into a famine zone by starving them. You prepare them by fattening them up, giving them calorie reserves so they have warmth to spare in the cold, lean times. And so I have prepared my child for an ugly world by fattening her with love, like a foie gras goose, fattened until its neck bursts, and I will catch the splattering goose fat too. And when we are sad, we sit there being sad, crying, accepting, until we laugh again. In our house, I have made sadness all right – it can come and go like familiar visitors do. I want to be the safe place my daughter turns to at night, and wakes up to in the morning. The safe harbour. Unconditional. Not everybody gets one of those.

One day we are sitting looking at an atlas on her bed. It transpires we should do this more often, because she thinks that Paris might be the capital of Spain and that she has definitely never ever *ever* heard of the capital city of Greece, even though she has heard of Athens. Things improve when we turn the page onto Eastern European countries that neither of us have ever been to. I still have questions though. 'Can you find me,' I say, pointing her somewhere vaguely in the direction of the Black Sea, 'a country whose capital city is almost my name?' Eventually she finds Sofia in Bulgaria. Full points.

'Now can you find me another city in that same country, but with a very funny name?' I ask.

She begins to read their names out.

'Ruse?'

'Oh, c'mon, Ruse isn't funny,' I say.

'Mmm. Varna?'

'Not funny.'

'Ta … Tar … Targovishte?' she wonders, trying to pronounce it.

'*Almost* funny,' I admit.

'Pleven!'

'All right, Pleven is quite funny,' I say, 'but no, there's a funnier one than Pleven. I think you've got your finger over it.'

She looks down.

'PLOVDIV,' she says, reading it out and cackling. 'PLOVDIV! PLOVDIV!' She thinks Plovdiv is the funniest place ever. She's squealing about Plovdiv. We are united in our love of Plovdiv, and I haven't even told her yet that I grew up near a Yorkshire village called Wetwang. I am enjoying this moment so much that I start missing it even while I'm still inside it. 'Plovdiv!' we shout, again and again until we have plovdivved ourselves into a frenzy, tickling each other right in the plovdivs. It is half past eight on a Friday night, and I don't know what they're doing in all the bars of Soho right now but I know it isn't half as funny as Plovdiv. One day, I think, I will pass my driving test, I'll get a car, her school will finish for the summer holidays and we'll drive all the way to Plovdiv, across the seas and the mountains and the borders. And we'll be hysterical. We'll plovdiv ourselves senseless the entire bloody way there.

34

My mother and I are more of a traffic island

I have been away on a work trip and my mum has been staying in my house looking after her grand-daughter. Now I'm back, we've put her to bed and she's asleep. The child, that is, not my mum, who has been awake for my entire life and all of hers too, and who, in the event of an apocalyptic global nuclear war would be one of three things to survive, the others being a) cockroaches and b) Cher. And yet I still want more of my mother's attention – specifically, I want her attention to fall upon all of the great and noble works that I do as a mother myself, and to praise me for them. She is not having this, however. Not for one single minute.

'We went to Westfield on the bus after school,' says my mum, sitting in my cream armchair with the holes in it that were made by a cat who once broke into our house and got bored. 'And I bought her a Lego kit with a house in it, but when we got home she said the house didn't have a proper kitchen so she made it a fridge with a glass door. A fridge! She made a little Lego fridge all by herself!'

'Oh yes, we do masses of Lego together,' I say, 'that's why I cleared the stuff off that Ikea cupboard thing and moved it to beside the sofa so I could turn it into a whole Lego town for her, she's been doing *loads* recently. It's been so great to watch her doing it, I mean, so great to do it all with her. Me with her together. Me.'

'And at school,' says my mum, warming to her theme, 'she doesn't mind going in the mornings, she actually seems to *like* going to school.'

'I know!' I say. 'She does really well, probably because we've done so much reading together, so she has such a good attitude towards it all, not perfectionistic, just enthusiastic and realistic and—'

'Well, you did well at school, too,' says my mother, but I do not take this as a compliment for me, I take this as a compliment for her, and thus discard it utterly.

'But *socially*,' says my mum, getting back to the more interesting topic, 'she has all of these friends in the playground, they all rush over to her the minute she walks in!'

'*Yes*,' I reply. 'She's a very happy and well-rounded person! The other children love her! It isn't an accident.'

By which I mean, she isn't an accident, not any more. By which I mean, I am the captain of this ship now, Mother, even if I never meant to go to sea. By which I mean, look how the boat did not sink, Mother, look how it did not sink, even though you were so very afraid when I was pregnant, and even though the Musician was so very afraid when I was pregnant, and even though, after I

233

moved back to England and sat in that little house in Piss Alley on my own, you came to stay there and you rubbed my big round belly, and as you rubbed it you said, 'Poor baby, poor *poor* baby,' in a tone of voice that I would recognise in a police line-up of tones of voices, even if I had recently become deaf.

We live in a different house now, quieter, near the park where I walk our dog every morning after taking my child to school. It was my mother who found the new house, and who helped us afford it. I am indebted to my mother. I can't tell where my mother ends and I begin any more.

'Daddy was so thrilled to hear that she actually likes maths now,' she carries on, not listening to the inside of my mind. 'All those times tables she can rattle off. I think he's a bit envious that I'm here and he's not. We just love her so much.'

'*YOU* LOVE HER! *YOU* LOVE HER! LAST WEEK YOU TOLD ME YOU LOVED MY DOG, MY ACTUAL FUCKING DOG, AND IT WAS THE FIRST TIME I HAD EVER HEARD YOU USE THE WORD "LOVE" IN RELATION TO A LIVING BEING, I SWEAR TO GOD I HAVE NEVER HEARD YOU SAY YOU LOVE ME OR MY BROTHER OR ANYONE ELSE AND NOW YOU SAY YOU LOVE MY DOG AND MY CHILD AND IF YOU'RE NOT WORKING UP TO THE GRAND FINALE WHEN YOU SAY YOU LOVE **ME** I'M GOING TO THROW THE DOG OUT OF THE WINDOW INTO THE PADDLING POOL THAT YOU BOUGHT US THAT

I DIDN'T EVEN ASK FOR JUST LIKE I NEVER ASKED TO BE BORN,' I reply.

Except that I don't.

I think about telling her that the first time anyone ever told me they loved me was when they were high on ecstasy, at a rave.

I don't.

Instead I say something about how I'm sorry Daddy has to go to the doctor's appointment on his own so she can be here looking after my child for me.

Or at least I think about saying that. What I actually say is that I am hungry, and she replies that she cooked supper before I got home and mine is in the oven for me to heat up, and so I go and do that, and I eat it in the kitchen while she watches the news in the sitting room, and I look over at some laundry she has done, my clothes, my daughter's clothes, and at some washing-up that she has done, our plates, our mess, and I have to admit that, while our relationship might not contain the word love, it does seem to contain a large number of things which look and taste an awful lot like it.

35

You never think about stopping, do you, Mummy?

'What did Yaya do when she had a job?' my daughter asks me. So I tell her that her grandmother was a social worker who worked with families with problems, like maybe the mum had a boyfriend who was secretly nasty to the children and the children hadn't been able to tell anyone, they needed another grown-up to come and help them. She takes this news quite well, nodding in an understanding fashion, as she reads gritty Jacqueline Wilson books now and goes to a school where some of the kids have felt that anger too. I have tried to gradually introduce her to the fact that the world isn't a safe place for everyone. I feel it's better to give her this news in dribs and drabs than to have it arrive in one big shock the day that somebody in the playground flattens her, or when she hears a description of actual war and torture for the very first time. Childhood needs a little tiny bit of badness, if only anecdotally. Life on Earth contains all of the things.

'And Yoyo, your grandad,' I tell her, 'was a university lecturer, which is like being a teacher but to older children, eighteen-, nineteen-, twenty-year-olds – and grown-ups too – who go to university after they've finished school. And he taught a subject called philosophy, and he special-ised in a part of that subject called philosophy of mind.' I know that she has no idea what I'm talking about, but it's also good to nonchalantly introduce batshit vocabulary to a seven-year-old sometimes.

'What is philoboby of mine?' she asks.

'Well,' I reply, wondering now why I decided to go down this route and put myself through this, 'philosophy of mind means thinking about thinking. Or maybe thinking about thinking about thinking.'

'Or maybe thinking about thinking,' she says, gasping for breath by her twenty-fourth thinking, and throwing herself onto my lap as if she were dead.

I suddenly remember how much I hate children.

'But then we invented the internet,' I say, 'and that put an end to all of that silly thinking.'

'I don't want to go to university,' she says, and suddenly I feel a small sense of dread gripping my stomach and a vision of my parents flashes in front of me, when I remember everything they must have gone through when

I said I didn't want to go either (a recurrent statement made between the ages of sixteen and thirty, even though I went many times.)

'You don't have to go!' I say brightly, with a false smile, my chest tightening as I realise I don't live outside the narrative at all, I'm just like any other middle-class mother-fucker in this joint and I want all the same things for her that the others do.

'I want to go to art school instead,' she says.

'OH!' I say, my middle-class heart leaping into the sky, 'well, that will be much more interesting, yes, go to art school!'

'But what if I don't get in?' she says, sounding a little anxious. I have absolutely no idea where she has found out about this stuff from. *Not getting in!* What fucker has been telling her this?

'Well, you just keep on painting those animals in your art classes on Wednesdays and working really hard on them and eventually your work will be good enough to get you into art school,' I reply. 'Just stick at it.'

'But what if I *still* don't get in?' she says, enjoying the dramatic tragedy of a hypothetical event that could possibly go wrong in ten years' time.

'Well then, you'll go there, and you'll bang on the door, and you'll tell them that they've made an absolutely terrible mistake and that they *have* to let you in,' I answer.

She looks at me as if this is perfectly right, and this is because we both know that she is a far more reasonable person than I am and thus she will never do any such thing whatsoever.

She says she wants some water, so I pour her some out of a jug and I carry on talking about how she could actually smash down the door of the art school, 'Mummy,' she says, but she needs to learn not to interrupt, so I carry on talking about how it's going to be harder if the door's made of metal but maybe she could take a soldering iron to burn her way through the lock, 'Mummy,' she says, and I try to remember if soldering irons can actually burn things apart or maybe they just join stuff together, 'MUMMY,' she says, and I am annoyed and I say *what*, and then I look at the glass.

It filled up several seconds ago and I have since been pouring water all over the table. She hasn't screamed like any other seven-year-old might do at this unexpected turn of events. Instead, she is looking at me with sympathy, like a mother might look upon her own child.

'Mummy,' she says, calmly. 'You never really think about stopping, do you?'

36

In which I ask Goldie Hawn
to rescue me

Goldie Hawn is eating scrambled eggs with ham when I walk into her hotel restaurant in London to interview her for a newspaper. She has to go on the Alan Carr television show later, and is wondering what to wear. She doesn't have as many clothes as she thought she did in her suitcase. I sit down on the other side of her table and order some tea from the waiter who clearly loves her, and who now has the exciting opportunity to pretend to love me too.

Goldie says she has been thinking about childhood, how when she was young she was so afraid that the Russians were going to bomb America and they were all going to die, there was all sorts of duck-and-cover propaganda in her school and she was a scared child, frightened to death. Now she has studied neurology and wants to teach children not to have such negative, fearful thoughts controlling them. She has invented a programme for kids to follow at school, to learn about mindfulness, and says that happiness is a cottage industry in America now, not like fifteen years ago when she first talked about this stuff and people looked at her as if she was crazy.

She is giving this interview because she has had such success teaching children to manage conflict with her mindfulness programme that she wants to push it out around the world, bring it to underprivileged kids everywhere. She teaches children to understand that the amygdala, which she describes as being like a funny little bulldog, is the part of the brain that is always on watch for a negative event, for any opportunity to think a bad thing is happening, because that is how it protects us, but the fact is there are no lions, tigers and bears out there and so we don't need this primitive brain so much now.

I am trying to nod at her as if I believe her about the lions, tigers and bears, and as if I am not crazy, even though I am currently – because life is a bit stressful and I get overwhelmed – feeling slightly crazy.

What we need, she says, is our thinking brain, our prefrontal cortex, which is the wise old owl who can come into play after we step back from the drama and breathe; take a mindful moment out. But negative thought after negative thought will continue, unless we learn how to stop the mind for a minute, and grab it. Learn to send the bulldog back to the doghouse.

It sounds great. Really great. I can't quite take it all in. I'm in the doghouse with my bulldog. Somehow we get through the whole interview. And then I hear a voice, and it is not Goldie's, it is mine, asking her one more question, which is, how she would deal with a child whose father had walked out when she was born, never to return? How could she talk to the child about him, and be sure to speak about him in a positive way, not fill the child's head with negative thoughts about this absent man?

'Oh. Well,' says Goldie, hmm, thinking about this, 'Well, let me see, well, first I would tell her that he loved her *very very much*, and that ...'

'No,' I interrupt, 'no, he didn't, he literally walked out, he didn't give himself the chance to love her, she was a tiny screaming baby and I don't think it's a good idea to tell her that people who love you can leave and never see you again.'

'Oh, oh I see, right, okay, let me think about this, this is a tricky one,' says Goldie Hawn.

Her taxi is waiting outside. She's already answered enough questions and it's time for her to leave.

'Because if I tell her that he's this wonderful guy and everything's cool,' I continue, 'then surely she's going to feel even more rejected – going to wonder even more about why he doesn't want to see her – you see, I made this one promise when he left – I told him I would never speak ill of him to our child, and I have absolutely kept it, I've honoured it so diligently and I've never said a bad word about him to her, and I never would, and she's a schoolgirl now, and all I've told her is that there is a man who helped me get pregnant when I wanted to have a baby, so she has a biological father in another country but not a daddy, because I was single, but the thing is now I'm thinking that maybe it would be healthier to explain that he actually *is* a bit of a fuck-up, you know, that he couldn't cope and he wasn't in the greatest of states, and then she knows it's not her fault, you know, maybe it's better to be a bit more realistic and explain that somebody in their right mind wouldn't do what he did …'

Goldie is listening.

'… but then somebody else told me that children think if their parent is bad then they themself must be bad, even if it's a parent they've never met, they have this sense that their absent father is half them and that that means there is a dark half inside them too, so, I don't know what to do.'

Goldie Hawn's beautiful big yellow hair is cushioning her increasingly perplexed face. She has to go. She knows that the interview time has run out and that I'm not even going to use this extra conversation in the article.

'Well look,' she says, clutching her handbag, 'you and I obviously have to talk about this more, so when I next come to London – you have my phone number, right?'

I tell her that no, I don't, because this meeting was arranged by her publicist and my editor and I just turned up at the appointed time – but, oh my heart! Goldie Hawn is going to save me! She's going to give me her number. I love her. Oh happy day.

Then she says, 'Oh.'

There is a pause. It is only a nanosecond's pause, but it is a nanosecond long enough for both Goldie Hawn and I to realise that there is no way the Oscar-winning actress and producer who is extremely busy running a global charity for people with genuine problems is going to give me her phone number. When will my mouth stop falling open, when will a cry for help stop falling out?

I can't tell you exactly what she said after that. I fiddled with turning the Dictaphone off. She said something like, well, we'll definitely have to stay in touch, and she hugged me and left and I sat right back down at her favourite table in the posh Kensington hotel and it washed over me, that feeling, flooding all around my body like ink from a shoplifting tag on a nice dress, or like piss all down my legs. That warm, familiar feeling of shame.

In the hotel, there was a pile of books that guests could borrow. I picked one up and read a poem by Rumi that had four lines in the middle of it which almost made me stop breathing:

Out beyond ideas of wrongdoing and rightdoing,
there is a field. I'll meet you there.
When the soul lies down in that grass,
the world is too full to talk about.

I had read Rumi years before, when I was a teenager who loved books but could barely concentrate enough to finish novels. Poetry had been my greatest love back then, my quickest fix, but it hadn't got me as deep in the guts as it did now. That field, that place beyond ideas of wrongdoing and rightdoing – I knew it. I had even *been* there in a dream, although it had come to me as a white room, which my father's daughter had walked into, grinning at me. In that dream we were friends again, and when I woke up from it I had felt lighter than I had done in years. It was better than language. I was free.

This was a man who had been straight with me from the day we met, years before any of this big stuff happened. Family life was not his path. Not because he didn't like children, but quite the opposite: because he thought children should have everything, a proper commitment. He wanted more for children than he felt he could give them; a rock-solid love that didn't come with so many ghouls. As far as I could see, he had spent so long fighting away the shadows in his own life that when the sun shone on it he ducked away from that too.

Since he had disappeared and we had stopped having any contact, my friends had of course said what a bastard he was. I tried to join in – believe me, I tried – but I couldn't bring myself to hate him. Beyond the noise of it all, beyond that world that was too full to talk about, I was quietly, bashfully grateful. He had given me my best ever present, in a curious pocket of magic that we had somehow slipped into through the Californian moonlight, and if I thought about what my life would have been without her – my diminutive partner in crime, and in beauty, and in fart jokes – I almost couldn't breathe again.

37

The Hungover Games

I went to see a therapist and told him about all of it: the partying, the panicking, the chaos. He listened. And he said a number of things, one of which was, you did it because you had never found a place of stillness inside yourself. I thought and thought about that sentence, and the sentence itself seemed to take me to that place that I had never had.

And I don't know exactly when my house became a nicer proposition than getting an actual proposition, but it happened. It crept in like a thief and now the pleasure of going out and overdoing it has gone. Maybe it's bad. Maybe I've died. Maybe, as my mother says, or rather hints, all of this is no substitute for a real relationship and I still need to try harder. Or maybe I've been to enough of my friends' lovely weddings to now be seeing them through their horrible divorces too, and watching them looking at my life and wondering if I wasn't right all along. If it wasn't a better set-up this way from the start. There is no right answer. But there isn't a totally wrong one either.

My daughter has missed out on several things; in other ways, she has been the queen of a wealthy country, and I think she might just miss the hungover games. The ones I invented to play with her specifically on a Saturday morning, when the babysitter had long since gone home, the nurseries were all closed, and it was just me and her, trying to find a way to play while my head throbbed with my stupidities from the night before. How we would creep to the local playground, where I had developed an amazing ability to make her think I was chasing her, round and round in a circle, all while I was in fact lying on the grass as still as possible, emitting squealing noises and occasionally waggling my arms in the air in an excited manner. How she would run and run to get away from me, the baddie chasing her, while I stayed exactly where I was, trying to look at Tinder on my phone.

Or the game where we wouldn't leave the house at all, if it was raining, and so I would lie very still on the floor, and let her and Teddy watch a video of lymphatic drainage massage on YouTube so they could practise pawing at my face and stroking my hair very very gently, being my doctors, and how she would tell Teddy and his soft paws that 'people are bears too, but with bones inside'.

Or perhaps she will miss the one where I now run her a warm bath and tell her about three witches who lived a long time ago, in a story by someone called Shakespeare, and how the witches would throw absolutely everything into their cauldron. So we throw everything into her bath that we can see, starting with the plastic toys that are supposed to be in it, and the sponges. Then comes a little more transgression, with the toothbrushes and the tubes of toothpaste, the cup they are kept in, some shampoo bottles with the lids on tightly if you don't mind, a hairbrush, a shower cap and an empty toilet roll tube to see what happens to cardboard in water. And then perhaps a page from the newspaper to see what happens to the ink. A couple of tangerines that we weren't going to eat anyway. A fifty-pence piece. A shoe.

We pour it all into the cauldron that is my daughter's bath, her yelps of delight turning into screams as she becomes surrounded by the naughtiest of objects that shouldn't be in there. I bring two wooden spoons from the kitchen for us to stir the water with, splashing ourselves everywhere, the floor is wet, my face is a dripping mess. And then on my phone, which I somehow keep far away enough from the water, I google the words to the three witches speech from *Macbeth* because I can only remember the first two lines, and I try to teach her the rest so we can shout out together 'Double double toil and trouble! Fire burn and cauldron bubble!' and then we throw in 'Wool of bat and tongue of dog!' Except my daughter is grabbing at the sounds of the words just as she is grabbing at all the stuff in her tub, so she bellows 'Scary dragon! Toothy woof!' instead of 'Scale of dragon' and 'Tooth of wolf' and the elements understand her perfectly. And she is always completely hysterical by the time I try to tell her that the witches are also known as the weird sisters, and that weird people are good, and witches are good, and maybe witches are just women whose power has been sat on for too long, burning up inside them like the fire that fuels the cauldron. I tell her, even though she can't hear me through her paroxysms of splashing, that I hope she learns to be a witch and find this power inside herself, this connection to the earth beneath her and the sky above. That I hope she grows perfumed thorns to put the cynics off the scent.

Nora Ephron wrote that she struggled terribly with being a girl, couldn't work out how to do it, how to be girlish, but that she made a pretty good woman. I struggled with being a girl and I also struggled with being a woman. But I make a damn fine witch.

38

In which I rescue myself

I had been starting to see my fortieth birthday as some kind of reckoning; a natural deadline imposed by biology, to make me stop and look around and breathe for a minute. A date that cannot be denied. You are young in your twenties, and you can now carry on that youth into your thirties, nobody really minds. You can even carry it on into motherhood, or so I seem to have managed. But forty. Fucking forty. You can't really take the piss when you're in your forties, can you? Not *all* the time.

You can't really send yet another email that goes 'oh my God can't believe I missed this thing you sent me for the third time two weeks ago' to one of Her Majesty's representatives from the Inland Revenue. You can't keep on being the one who entertains your married friends with your hilarious dating disasters before leaving them to plan tomorrow's dinner of lobster while you go home and sob into your Super Noodles. You can't spend two hours arguing about absolute bobbins with absolute strangers in full public view on Twitter, only to go mysteriously offline for the next forty-eight hours when a magazine editor emails you to ask about the work you said was definitely nearly finished 'just tidying it up, all the word count is there', a week ago.

When you're forty, I tell myself, you can't run out of clean knickers and then go through them all again wearing them inside out and then move on to your bikini and then wear your bikini inside out too, all to avoid the heady conflagration of mental challenges and bureaucratic demands that is known as 'putting a wash on'. The rampant discomfort of wearing inside-out bikini bottoms beneath your tights is just a stretch too far for a forty-year-old woman, I have been telling myself. You can't keep doing things while pretending that you're not doing them. You can't keep living a temporary lifestyle on a permanent basis. This has to *stop*.

Because forty-year-old women do not send their children to school with a bag of clothes that look 'a bit *like* your PE uniform' because they can't find the PE uniform again, or insist, because they literally never have any cash on them and exist solely on credit cards, that the ice-cream van only plays that music 'when it has run out of ice cream'. I know this has to change. I know.

And the place to have this sort of reckoning is not, I suspect, in an all-inclusive beach resort in Jamaica, but by some jamminess that is where I have been asked to spend my fortieth birthday, to write a travel article about a high street package holiday company that is trying to posh up its image. I won't be with any of my friends for this trip, just travel reps, but the thought of that sunlight and that sea is intoxicating, even if I am going to spend a full day travelling out there, two nights in the hotel and then another day coming back. They won't pay for a flight for my daughter too, which means I have to ask my mum if she can come to London and babysit. Again.

On the one hand, she will be glad that the universe has somehow conspired to give me a mini-holiday to Jamaica for my fortieth birthday, as this is a very nice thing to happen to me. On the other hand, she will be absolutely livid that the universe has somehow conspired to give me a mini-holiday to Jamaica for my fortieth birthday, as this is a very nice thing to happen to me. It is not that my mother wants me to live a life without niceness, but she would certainly like my allotted amount of the stuff to come from a more sustainable source, such as my proving able to commit myself to a normal relationship with a normal man and all the boredom and frustration that that might well entail and then maybe we could book some holidays of our own and take our own child with us. I'm just saying.

Sorry, I meant to say *love* – my mother surely wants me to have all the love and support as well as the boredom and frustration that such a relationship might well entail. Not a life in which I muddle along as a single parent, punctuated by my ridiculous job interviewing celebrities and the occasional free holiday that I don't have to organise or pay for and that lasts as many hours on the plane as on the beach – well, when I ring my mother up and ask her to babysit, and she says 'Hmmmmm,' there are fathoms, so many deep fathoms in her hmm, that I have already lived a lifetime inside each of them.

And all right, maybe it makes me feel a bit stupid too, that it's a travel company and an editor at work who have asked me to go on this trip, and not somebody who loves me. Maybe it's weird that they didn't even know the significance of the date and that I will spend my fortieth flying through the air, alone. Maybe I feel like a prize numpty having to ask my own mummy if I'm even allowed to go. Maybe I should have followed her advice years ago, and settled, just settled for someone, accepted a different kind of life. 'They're *all* boring,' she said, the last time this properly came up, 'you just have to pick one and get on with it. You just *settle*,' she said, and I had in fact forgotten my father was in the room at this moment, but not for much longer, because he piped up and said, while nodding sagely, 'I always knew that, to your mother, I was a settlement,' and then he added, muttering, 'somewhere off the coast of Nova Scotia.'

On the flight over, alone, I get chatting to the young woman sitting next to me. She works in PR. She's young and blonde and beautiful. We get quite far into our life stories, in that way you can only do if you've had a gin and tonic at 40,000 feet and the earth is scuttling past beneath you like a sheepish spider, while the clouds claim you as their new friends, and there's just been a particularly terrorising run of turbulence. God, I love turbulence.

It's all right – I have learned, now, that turbulence makes other people scared. I have learned that it is wise to pretend to be sympathetic about other people being scared by turbulence, but this is still very strange to me, because

253

turbulence is just about the only thing that calms my mind, that makes me feel safe. I'm a good flyer anyway, a much more relaxed person in the air than on the land, but I'm even better when the air gets rough. Honestly, when the plane starts shaking and the seatbelt signs come on, like a warm embrace from some particularly demented gods, it's about the only time when my outside matches my inside. I exhale.

So after it finishes I talk to the beautiful young thing next to me. Her boyfriend has got two young kids from when he was married, just babies, really. He lives in a different house from his kids, but in the same town, a European city, but he's moving to London soon to be with this woman, and he'll still visit the kids all the time and they'll come over all the time too, and it'll be good for everyone really, better, less stress, because his ex-wife is *crazy*.

Really, I say, extending one eyebrow into fantasy land, from where I can see every woman who has ever been called crazy. Every woman who ever went through a relationship with a man who found out having kids was difficult, found out that freedom was difficult, found out that the anger of the female body in a world built for men was difficult, and who left that woman for a younger woman who didn't give him all that hassle because she was full of sunshine not resentment in the mornings, and who now gets to absolve himself of any guilt by saying that his ex is *crazy*!

Because it is my fortieth birthday I do not keep all these thoughts inside my head at the expense of offending my new friend. I actually say them, out loud, much to her surprise. There, that feels better. I knock back another slug of the complimentary G&T. I'm a grown-up now.

The next morning I look in the mirror in my Jamaican hotel room at the forty-year-old in a bikini who is standing there. It is 7 a.m. For the launch of this new hotel they have invited a supermodel, who I have to go and meet a bit later, down on the white sands. She will also be in her bikini, of course, which is great, absolutely great, no problems there. She'll probably ask me for tips. No, but, what with me being a grown-up now, finally, I have to admit that this body I've been lugging around for some time isn't just the replacement one I'm using until my real one gets out of the menders. There was only ever one body, and there was only ever one life. And this is it.

But before that I'm out of the door, I'm straight into that sea, and I'm floating. And then I swim right out until I stop being forty and flobbly, and become pure form, a body made largely of water meeting a larger body of water, a bright bolt of aquamarine. I think about my daughter and how much she would be giggling if she was in this sea with me right now, splashing the water into my eyes to remind me that she exists, again and again and again, while I'd be screaming at her to stop, and then we'd both be falling about crying laughing at each other, spluttering, choking.

I swim farther out and think about everything. I think about how I am the product of two people who fucked and fought and loved each other. So is my daughter, when it comes down to it. And so it goes, and all of human life really is a great big Jacob's Ladder of generations, of people falling into the next and the next, people lusting after each other, people fighting, shouting, loving, losing, crying and starting all over again, and there isn't much that you can do about it, except dive in, to where you find the deepest blue. I think about how I've been looking for a father figure for her since the day she was born, frantic to find somebody else to make sense of us, to love us. I wonder, out in this clear blue ocean, why it has taken me so much longer to notice that there is more than enough love already. That the picture is already complete.

So I swim out to sea. Maybe too far out, I should probably stop. You never think about stopping, do you, Mummy. The thing is, though, I've been out at sea for most of my life – and the water has always been so deep, so blue, so lovely.

Acknowledgements

To my dad and my brother for being the best of men, for scooping my daughter up, and for showing me at a young age that books can take you everywhere. If my writing is at all funny then that's something I learned from you, Daddy. And to Nicola Henson, my best friend from school days, as I've just found out that we're on another dissident journey together – I could not be happier for you and the duff that you're up.

Diane Burns for always having my back, my front and my other parts, Loulou Androlia for being my soft rock, Chandra Haabjoern for your unwavering love, King Uncle Rory Phillips for being a real pal and to Erol Alkan for bringing all of us together at a club called Trash in the first place. Part of the weekend never dies, especially on Mondays.

To my ladies of the canyon in LA: my beloved Mandy Kahn, as well as Ki Ellwood, Kathryna Hancock, Tabitha Denholm, Molly Hewitt and Ioanna Gika, thank you for everything you have done for me and her. Not forgetting Anna Sussman in New York – we made it throoough the wilderness.

London: To Hannah May and Lois, Gemma Tortella and Sofia and May, oh my god I'm so glad you all exist. You will always represent our salvation and our fun.

Rebecca Schiller: thank you for the generous loan of your sanity. You can have it back now.

Big love also to Eva Wiseman, Sasha Nixon, Matilda Tristram, Rachel Roberts, Kate Moross, Will Bramley, Phil Beeken, Damien Doorley, Dan Foat, Joy Lo Dico, Nine Yamamoto, Georgie Okell, Cibelle Bastos, Colin Roberts, Robert Ninot, Michael Serwa, Gemma

Cairney, Jesse Darling, Katy Stevenson Bretton, Hazel Mayes, Miranda Bowen and Chambers Restaurant on Lauriston Road E9 for all the chips that my child has eaten. So many chips. And Love Bike Thai Kitchen in Dalston for all the pad Thai, and the Starbucks in Golders Green for all the sausage sandwiches that went into this book, via me. Hermione Hodgson, you take the loveliest author photos – and still nobody has noticed the dog.

Polly and David: thank you for having me to stay and then ignoring me so I could finally write the whisper that would become this story. The impossible turned into the possible that day. And to Melanie Eclare's family, Rose and Tom Petherick, for taking my phone and my child off me and providing yet more sanctuary. Stories Books & Cafe in Echo Park you are my favourite place on Earth; Skylight Books in Los Feliz you are a close second.

People talk about sisterhood a lot, and rightly so, but some of the greatest kindness to me as a single mother has come from men and I will never forget it. Josh Frankfort googling folic acid and driving me to Whole Foods the minute I said I was pregnant. Rob Fitzpatrick turning up with a cot and a changing table. Diego Tellez coming round to build my flatpack bed after the van driver incident. Dan Trilling bringing Friday night takeaways after the baby was born, and doing the washing up; your politics are personal and it shows. Myles Macinnes for taking the child to the park so I could read the newspaper; those Sunday mornings number among the most precious moments of my life. Kev Kharas and Alex Miller for letting me write what I really wanted to – I'd never known such freedom in words. Greg Barrett for never failing to ask if I could come to the pub. Uncle Nick for something similar. And the brilliant Babak Ganjei for being the only other single parent in the village.

To everyone who helped with babysitting, teaching and cleaning: sorry about all the mess I really will clear it up soon. Hannah McCarthy, Ana Florentina, Caitlin Findlay, Eglantina Mema, Sherine Graham, Noel Basualdo, Magalie Billaud: you all saved my arse.

Thanks to my editor Bea Hemming, for your calm, wise unflappableness, and the greatest thanks of all to my agent Georgia Garrett for gently nursing this book to light through all of my angst: you are superhuman and yet so very human too.

And finally, to the nursery teacher who said that my daughter, aged two and a half, was 'too exuberant' and should wear fewer bright colours and more grey, may I suggest a long and sexual holiday.